I AM > I WAS

FROM IDENTITY LOST TO PURPOSE FOUND

by
Lo-Ammi Richardson

Published by Watersprings Publishing, a division of
Watersprings Media House, LLC.
P.O. BOX 1284
Olive Branch, MS 38654
www.waterspringsmedia.com
Contact publisher for bulk orders and permission requests.

Copyrights © 2020 by LoAmmi Richardson

All rights reserved. No part of this publication may be reproduced, distributed, or transmitted in any form or by any means, including photocopying, recording, or other electronic or mechanical methods, without the prior written permission of the publisher, except in the case of brief quotations embodied in critical reviews and certain other noncommercial uses permitted by copyright law.

Printed in the United States of America.

Library of Congress Control Number: 2020921049

ISBN-13: 978-1-948877-63-3

TABLE OF CONTENTS

Introduction 1

CHAPTER 1 Born A Mistake! 3

CHAPTER 2 A Different World 11

CHAPTER 3 The Return 26

CHAPTER 4 Selection Day 43

CHAPTER 5 Who Am I? 49

CHAPTER 6 Dream Chasing 62

CHAPTER 7 I'm Back! 74

CHAPTER 8 What Is The Meaning of Life? 808 And Heartbreaks 84

CHAPTER 9 Dead and Gone 90

CHAPTER 10 If They Could Only See Me Now! 101

About The Author 108

ACKNOWLEDGEMENTS

This book is dedicated to everyone who believed in my vision throughout the years, the ones who pushed me and never made me stop believing in myself. Just know that you have been my rock in helping me accomplish this major goal of mine. To everyone who has supported me through prayers and finances, thank you! Your encouraging words helped me when I felt like giving up. Your voice helped me press forward. To my brother, mentor, and friend, Taurus Montgomery, thanks for planting this book idea in my heart. As I journey on this new venture, I'm forever grateful, bro! To Andrew and Melanie Roquiz, what can I say? We did this! Without your help, this would have never happened. I find it funny we didn't know what we were doing throughout this process, but we stuck with it and accomplished something we all can be proud of. Words cannot begin to describe my gratefulness and your dedication to this project. To my pain, my hurt, my mistakes, and my past, thank you! Without you, I would not be who I am today!

INTRODUCTION

Lo-Ammi! what a unique and awkward name for a child. Why would anyone name their child Lo-Ammi? My name given to me at birth fit perfectly to my childhood experience, awkward and out of place. Little did I know the significance my name would play in my life's journey. My name perfectly described the root to my problem in trying to find myself, where I fit in, my purpose in life, and my identity. The name Lo-Ammi comes from a story found in the book of Hosea. Lo-Ammi is the name of a child who reflected a nation in regards to their relationship with their God.

Lo – means not
Ammi – means my people

Throughout most of my life, I wasn't the person I was created to be. Everyone knew me as Lo. As I ventured in discovering my purpose and identity, my name reflected my destiny.

It wasn't until I came to the realization of who I was created to be that I later understood the meaning of *Ammi*. I now know who I am, whom I was created to be, and what my purpose is in life. I hope that you too will find your own path and journey, but most importantly, discover your identity through reading my story. I was lost, but now I can truly live by the name *Ammi*. My people!

Through this book, I want you to find yourself just like I did. I want to give you hope and let you know that who you were yesterday doesn't have to be who you are now. May my book help you discover your purpose in life, identify your calling, and most importantly help you find your identity.

Every life lived has a purpose. Yours has a great one. You can find it if you keep in mind...

I am > I was.

CHAPTER 1

BORN A MISTAKE!

"You're a mistake!" Those were the last words I heard from my father as I was being handcuffed and taken away to the juvenile detention center. I wasn't the best teenager growing up. However, in my defense, all I was trying to do was figure out life, who I was, and how to fit in.

The night's events replayed through my mind as I sat on the uncomfortable black leather seat in the back of the police car. Cold metal handcuffs etched against my wrists, but I barely noticed because I was distracted by my dad's gruff voice playing like a broken record inside my head. *You're a mistake. You're a mistake. You're a mistake.* The record wouldn't quit playing. I just couldn't shut that phrase off.

I knew I wasn't planned. Nobody at retirement age plans on having a baby. My parents were no exception. When I was born, my mom was 45, and my dad, or *Pops* as I sometimes called him, was 61. My pop's words that day unveiled my true feelings. I was a mistake. I wasn't planned. I wasn't supposed to be. I knew all of this, and I felt it with every bone in my body. As a result, my mind was never at ease. Questions constantly bombarded my mind regarding my place in this world. *If I was a mistake, then, who am I? What is life all about? What is my purpose?* I needed answers.

Hartford, Connecticut, once the richest city in the U.S., was where I was born. At the age of six months, my family and I made the big move to Puerto Rico. My mom was Puerto Rican, so this move took her back to her roots. My dad, born and raised in Massachusetts, was Black. I was born a mutt. That's me, the mutt, a biracial kid, torn between two worlds and cultures. When I hung around Blacks, they would tell me I was Puerto Rican. When I hung around Puerto Rican people, they would tell me I was Black. I was like a misfit puzzle piece, confused about where I belonged. *What was I?*

Because I moved to Puerto Rico at such a young age, my memories of Connecticut came solely from the stories and baby pictures my mom would share. I recall seeing pictures of myself leaning on the TV trying to trace letters during Wheel of Fortune. Other photos featured my home with a garage that had maroon floors and a kiddie pool in the front yard. However, none of these were actual memories of mine, just precious moments captured on camera.

Of the memories that I do own, many of them involve my parents arguing. Though my parents loved each other, it didn't stop them from fighting. They argued a lot. It was a constant memory of mine growing up with them.

One particular argument remains engraved into my mind. God-knows-what my parents were arguing about this time, but it was bad enough that it left a knot on my forehead the size of a potato. There my parents stood in the middle of the living room pissed off at each other. They were caught up in a heated exchange of words. I was hiding behind the coffee table. I have no idea how I got there, but there I was stuck between my parents going at each other. As the argument escalated, I tried to intervene. When all of a sudden, my mom, frustrated with my dad, grabbed the large potato-sized rock that she used as a doorstop, and threw it at him. Except, she missed, and it hit me.

When my parents argued, it caused me much pain. In the case of the rock, it was literal pain, but most of the time, the pain was emotional. Most of my parents' arguments had to do with money. And when money wasn't the cause, *then I was* – at least that's what I thought. After all, it made sense, my entrance into this world wasn't planned. So, logically, me, the growing thorn of issues in their side, was to blame. Little did I know how off my logic really was. These problems stemmed from my parents' own issues that had nothing to do with me.

It took me years to understand that the unresolved issues between them negatively affected me, but it wasn't because of me.

Despite the arguments, and the hospital visit due to the rock-on-forehead incident, I knew that my parents loved me. I loved them too. Their love was apparent because they expressed it through their own love languages – hugs, kisses, and money. The unfortunate part was that hugs and kisses, though appreciated, wasn't what I needed most at that time. My needs were entirely different, but my parents had no clue what those needs were. I just needed to be heard.

I needed someone to take the time to listen to me, to understand me, to help me troubleshoot through my insecurities. I needed someone to help me to discover who I was and my place in this world.

Growing up, I tried my best to get along with my parents, but it didn't always work. My world was so foreign to my parents because of the simple fact that it had drastically changed since they were young. The movies in my parents' days were black and white, and their worldview. Their world was completely detached from mine and their counsel disconnected with my reality. All this left a lot of friction between us, especially between my dad and me.

To give my parents credit, they tried in their own ways to connect with me. Mom taught me lessons from the Bible. Both my mom and dad enjoyed sharing with me stories of their upbringing. Though I would attentively listen to them, none of their teachings or stories made much sense. Growing up, many unanswered questions regarding my identity and purpose lingered in my mind. Yet, I felt as if I had no one to seek answers and advice from. Therefore, at the end of the day, I felt abandoned to make my own decisions and figure out life on my own.

Mom and Dad were both religious people and made sure that religion was a priority at home. We attended an all-black Caribbean church. I was the light-skinned, big-eared, and bucktoothed boy who looked different from everybody else. Everyone at my church looked, acted, and even thought very different from me. The culture, the environment, the people–all of it I did not understand. I still kept wondering, *who am I? How do I fit in?*

To make things worse, my speech wasn't the best. I have home videos of my younger self stuttering and stammering over my words. My mom only spoke to me in Spanish, and my dad only in English. Research shows that growing up in a bilingual home has its benefits. Some even argue that children from bilingual homes tend to adapt better to changing environments. Well, that wasn't me, for sure. No benefits in sight. Just added confusion, and more reasons to wonder...*Who the heck am I? Am I supposed to be Spanish speaking like my mom? Or Black like my dad?*

Despite the fact that I grew up feeling misplaced, and confused, I still turned out to be a rather independent person. My dad worked long hours, so I was often left to my lonesome to do anything I pleased. That's probably how I developed this stubborn mind of my own. Once my mind was set on doing a particular thing, no one could tell me otherwise. I just did my thing. Because of this, I hated authority figures. Not just my dad, anyone.

One late evening, I was sitting in my pop's room using the computer. Being that it was the only computer we owned, he decided to keep it in his room. I wasn't usually the type of student to be on top of schoolwork, but for whatever reason, I wanted to get this particular assignment done. So, there I was, focused, trying to knock out this assignment. While in the zone, my dad busts into the room and asks, "Did you use the bathroom?"

"Yup," I replied quickly trying not to break the zone I was in.

"Well, you didn't flush the toilet!" he yelled back. "You need to get up and flush the toilet!"

"I will, as soon as I finish typing this last paragraph!"

"No," he said with an aggravated voice, "you need to get

up and do as I told you to do!"

"Ugh…. Dad…— articulating each word with precision, as if I was clapping each word with my hands…soon…as…I'm…done….WRITING THIS PARAGRAPH!" Then, without hesitation, Pops yanks the computer cord. My screen goes black. All my work. Gone. Just like that. Ticked off, I stepped up to his face, yelling "Why the H*%# did you do that?" Seconds later, my dad tries to snatch a nearby belt to beat me with it. Pops must have forgotten that I wasn't a kid anymore. As we were scuffling, Pops swung the belt at me, and then, WHACK! Immediately, I felt a sting on my lip.

At that point, I snapped. Pissed off, I put my pops to the ground. All I wanted to do was punch the old man. It's as if my dad could read my thoughts because fear was in his eyes. Releasing my hold on him, I got up, walked over to the phone and called the police because I didn't know what either he or I was going to do next. A few moments later, those red and blue lights showed up at our front door. The moment the cops arrived all the questioning began. I lied when they asked me about my busted lip and blamed the injury on basketball. I'm not exactly sure what my dad told the police that night because even though I called the police, I was the one they chose to handcuff.

Standing in the middle of the room in handcuffs, I glanced at my dad who was sitting just inches away in the kitchen staring right at me. There he was, hands crossed, and shaking his head with disapproval. Then I hear these words, "You're a disappointment."

"Pops, tell mom where I am going," I shout across the room.

"I'm not tellin' her nothin'!" Pops continues to shake his head. "You're a mistake."

That evening's ugly altercation wasn't about measly chores versus some goliath assignment. Digging beneath the surface, it was really about my hurts, my pains, my frustrations. My lack of identity, the challenges I experienced due to my upbringing, all made me feel a certain way--a way so unsettling it triggered behavior that led me to be arrested that night.

My parents and I may not have always gotten along, or seen eye-to-eye, but one thing I did recognize was that they always made sacrifices for me. Something that I noticed is they were excellent at making sacrifices for my materialistic needs. Yet, when it came to dealing with their own personal issues, such as their marriage and parenting, they lacked the foresight in understanding that these unresolved issues would result in greater problems in the future.

My parents' problems soon got the best of them, and they ended up separating sometime during my pre-teen years. It's a wonder how those two even got together in the first place or how they were even attracted to each other. My mom loved gardening, found pleasure in cooking, deemed cleaning as fun, treasured the country, but always enjoyed the finer things in life. She would often share stories about her childhood growing up in Morovis, Puerto Rico and how much simpler life was back then. Pops, on the other hand, was a blue-collar worker, who enjoyed sharing riddles, singing jingles, and watching TV. He was a city slicker who was known as "Shaky Rich" aka "Shakespeare" when he was a teenager. He earned these names for the countless number of love poems he wrote. Perhaps it was the magic of the poems that made my mom fall for him. Who knows! Different as they were, they still managed to conceive me.

When my parents met, their differences were already obvious. However, their differences became more pronounced as their marriage continued and both had to live in places they weren't accustomed to. After living in Puerto Rico for some time, my parents decided to move to Florida. It was agreed that my dad would stay behind and live in the house in Puerto Rico until it sold. My dad, who wasn't originally from Puerto Rico, had fallen deeply in love with the beautiful island. No one thought that he'd ever leave. My mom found a house in Florida and took me with her, and we both waited for the house to sell.

No one expected the house to sell quickly, but somehow he did it, and before we knew it, my dad moved to Florida with us. Because of the unresolved issues between my parents, years later, my mom decided to return to Puerto Rico. Imagine trying to live through that experience of bouncing back and forth on airplanes just to be with either one of your parents. The moving was like a seemingly endless saga of hot potato (pun intended), leaving me as the new kid on the block, with many unanswered questions. My search for identity never seemed to end. That's me. The half Black, half Puerto Rican, who understood Spanish yet couldn't speak it. That's me, the kid who lived in the country, yet had city boy tendencies, and had a genuine bucktoothed smile that masked the pain coming from a broken home. I was seeking to discover purpose in life and place in this world. Yes, this was me, Lo-ammi, the lost, and confused kid, who always wondered….

Who Am I?

This is a common question most people ask themselves at some point in their lives. *What's my purpose? What's my calling? What was I put on this earth for?* Growing up, I would repeatedly ask myself these same questions too. I labeled myself as a mistake and was searching for my identity in hope to come across some answers.

I've often aimed to "live young, be wild, act free"– a simple mantra the world often encourages individuals to live by. However, beneath the surface of this mantra, rest many unanswered questions. How can one do this? Can you really live and act free while not knowing who you are, and what you were created to be?

If you find yourself like me, perhaps seeking answers to life's many questions, struggling to fit in, searching for identity, or maybe experiencing trials and heartache, take heart, you aren't alone.

Through reading my story, my desire is to give you hope. May you discover that despite rough moments in life, there is a silver lining. You too can discover the answer to this big question...

QUESTIONS

- Who Am I?
- What questions have you asked yourself about life?
- Do you struggle with finding your purpose and identity? If so, has it contributed to who you are today?
- Who do you feel you were created to be?

CHAPTER 2

A DIFFERENT WORLD

Why am I here? It wasn't even my choice! Angry thoughts raced through my mind as I sat in the backseat of a 1995 green Mitsubishi Montero. Around the corner, Reggaetón blasted from speeding cars as the loud mufflers rattled through the roads. I enjoyed the beat to the music, but I couldn't figure out what they were saying. *This is far different from the rap music that I was accustomed with.*

Gazing out the backseat window, I took in at the scenery passing before me. The roads were busy with bumper to bumper traffic. People were on each corner selling water bottles, newspapers, and ice cream. *Man, this is nothin' like home.* I tilted my head back into my seat because I was feeling nauseous during our car ride through the curvy mountain roads. After what seemed like an eternity, we finally turned the corner and slowly drove past one of the largest bars in town. Both young and old alike were there, simply passing time, drinking, playing pool, and hanging out next to an old juke box playing old classic salsa and Merengue music. Our car began to slow down and finally came to a halt at a white-gated green-walled house that my mom called home. Thoughts lingered in my mind. *I can't believe I have to live here now!*

My parents were separated, and up until this time, I had been living with my dad in Orlando. I was a Florida boy, but now I felt like an outsider in the small island of Puerto Rico. To make matters worse, my new home, Morovis, was known as one of the most country-like cities. When I'd mentioned to others that I lived in Morovis, I'd typically get this one response, "Oh, you live there in the mountains!"

Morovis had no McDonalds (I was there when they opened the first one, and it was the talk of the town). There were no fancy malls or super-highways. In addition to all this, our house had no AC or cable – far different from my home in the States. To make matters worse, my mom didn't drive, which meant that we had to be dependent on other people to get around. Our home was on a busy intersection, where semi-trucks and motorcycles loudly drove by in front of my front porch. For a *country town*, it sure wasn't a quiet place. Morovis was definitely no Orlando, Florida.

Morovis, though strange as it was, wasn't exactly foreign to me. During the past few years, I had traveled to Morovis to visit my mom during the summer months. So, its uniqueness was familiar to me. However, those summer visits were different. They felt like vacations. For starters, they were vacations. All those visits were temporary, so it was easy to let whatever inconveniences I experience slide. Second, the island did have its perks. Puerto Rico is absolutely beautiful. It has stunning beaches and lush rainforests. The people are lively, the culture is unique, and the food of course is bomb! Plus, I also enjoyed attending the Titanes de Morovis professional basketball games. It's a team with such rich history, and because of that, I could never pass an opportunity to watch them play. It was always fun to listen to stories that friends and family would share about the team during the time it was at its peak. Summer visits to Morovis were one thing, but to live there?! Now, that was a different story!

This time around was different. I wasn't on a vacation anymore. I was here to stay. Plus, it wasn't even my choice to move! I felt tricked, trapped, and out of place. I wasn't a *Jibaro* (country boy) as they would say in Puerto Rico. I did not belong. Morovis was a place so far out of my comfort zone. I wanted to leave and return to Florida to live with my dad. What made matters worse was that no one even seemed to care about my pent-up feelings of anger.

How I ended up getting tricked into moving to Morovis is

a story all by itself. It all began with me getting played by my pops. It was afternoon time, sometime during the summer of '97, right before the start of my 7th grade year. I was snooping around my dad's room and stumbled across plane tickets to Puerto Rico. There was nothing unusual about finding the plane tickets because we did visit Puerto Rico quite often.

I read through the ticket details and noticed that something was off. My dad's ticket was a round trip, and mine was a one-way. *What's up with that?!* I walked out of the room to ask why.

"What's up with my one-way ticket?" I questioned.

"Don't worry about it," he responded, "I'll purchase your return trip before school starts."

His response should have been a red flag to me, but I ignored my skepticism because I figured there was no reason to doubt him. After all, in my mind, my dad's reasoning made some sort of sense. So, I brushed off the ticket situation and went about my business.

Summertime rolled by, and the day came for us to use those tickets. We headed to the airport, checked in our bags, and made it to the gate. Once we arrived in Puerto Rico, we visited family, went out to eat, and toured some beautiful Puerto Rican sites together with family and friends. Two weeks into this "supposed visit," my dad returned to Orlando, while I stayed back in Puerto Rico for the remainder of the summer. Things were going as planned, or so I thought.

As the summer drew to a close, I was anxious to return home to Orlando. Anticipating the start of the school year, I called my dad and reminded him that school registration was around the corner and drew his attention to the list of items that needed to be completed. I was expecting our conversation to end with something like, "Okay, will do. Oh, yeah, and your ticket is set for you to leave Puerto Rico at such and such a date." But what happened next caught me off guard.

"You aren't coming back to Florida. You are staying in Puerto Rico with your mother," Pops harshly stated over the phone.

Confused, I asked, "What?! What do you mean I'm stayin' with mom? I thought I was going back to Orlando. That's what you told me."

"Nope. You don't listen! You are nothin' but a headache!" he exclaimed, commanding me to hand the phone to my mother who was standing beside me.

He lied to me! This was his plan the whole time, for me to stay in Morovis! I was pissed. Total betrayal. I tried to get my mom to speak on my behalf and convince my dad to let me return to Orlando. However, the more I begged her to do so, the more she showed disinterest in what I had to say. Instead, she did the opposite, and tried to persuade me to stay with her! My parents wouldn't budge on their decision. I was so ticked off about all that just happened. So many thoughts were running through my head. I couldn't deny the hurt I felt at that moment, but at the same time, I was trying to find answers to the questions that came after that conversation. *What did I do? Why did my parents lie to me? Why do I have to live here? I don't speak Spanish! There is nothing here for me! No AC, no TV, and the worst part of it is…. I have no friends to connect with.*

The story gets worse. The next week, I overheard my parents speaking over the phone. The conversation was a bit muffled, but I still overheard my mom say, "He is staying here with me. So, please make sure to have the money sent to me."

I was pissed. *What? Am I nothing more than a mere paycheck? Am I just extra pension for my retired parents? Is this all about money?! And what?!* The baffling part was that my mom agreed on this too! I expected this kind of activity from my dad, but not my mom! My mom was usually honest and transparent with me, but this time she wasn't, which is the part that hurt me the most. That day I felt reduced to nothing more than a dollar sign. I had just gotten played by my very own parents.

Later, my mom tried to mend the situation by explaining the benefits of living in Puerto Rico, like that was supposed to help! I could only focus on the fact I was lied to. End of story.

It's possible that my dad's assessment of me was correct. Maybe I was a headache and had a listening problem. He may have been right, but in my mind, all my actions were justified.

Why listen to my dad when he didn't listen to me? What's the point in behaving? After all, I'm just a cash-grab-in and a check to whoever claims me.

In retrospect, if I hadn't been a constant pain to my dad, he probably wouldn't have tricked me. But the truth is, I purposely rebelled and chose to be a pain to him. It was hard to identify it then, but looking back, I realize that my misbehavior was all just a cry for help--a cry for help because I felt controlled. A cry for help because I struggled with finding my identity. A cry for help because the emotional connection between me and my dad was lacking. A cry for help because I felt that dad chose work over me and was not present when I needed him.

The rebellion and mischief that led me out of Orlando and to Morovis began with "little things" that were all done to fill a slowly growing void inside me. These *little things* were nothing crazy, but rather simple activities that normal teens would do. You know, the average teen stuff such as staying up late, watching rated R movies, and listening to inappropriate music. However, in time, I found myself wanting to do more than just the *little things*.

My dad wanted me to move to Puerto Rico because of these *things* such as this next story. One evening, when living in Orlando, one of my older friends invited me to a teen club. I had never been to a teen club before, so I was hyped at the opportunity, yet nervous at the same time. At that time, I was still rather sheltered, and was new to the club scene. I may have appeared a bit awkward and corny, but that didn't matter or stop me from anything. That night, I did everything to try to fit in, and actually somewhat managed to succeed. I know this because I ended up having a blast! Everything about that evening was so empowering–the music, the beautiful girls, and experiencing my first dance. The thrill and fulfillment of staying out late with my boys that evening made me feel important and connected. It was an addicting feeling I knew I couldn't let go of. So, I went out, again, and again, and again.

I was so desperate to feel connected and to fit in. I did everything to make that possible. From clubbing, to how I dressed, and how I talked, all was done in an effort to belong. I know my boys would think to themselves, "Really dude? You doin' da most!" when they saw me do the things I did.

I did some wild stuff such as taking my father's car while he was at work and joyriding with one of the neighborhood kids. We did this without a license. Stealing basketball cards from local gas stations became an afternoon hobby. One time my friend and I even took a gun to the back of the woods near our house and emptied the clip. We did not even consider that someone could be walking along straight into our path. Thankfully no one was killed or injured. These are just a few of the *things* we did for nothing but pure enjoyment.

It is only because my dad worked nights, which left me unsupervised, that I was able to do all these crazy things. However, my situation quickly changed the day dad decided to retire again. My dad's home presence suddenly accelerated from zero to one hundred overnight. He went from merely being my chauffer to school to attempting to be my own personal security guard. Dad was observant. He quickly noticed some specific habits of mine (staying up late, leaving the house late at night, having company over etc...) and decided to enforce strict rules. Of course, I rarely complied with his rules. Actually, the more he enforced them, the more I rebelled. So yes, he probably saw me as a wild kid and deemed me as a pain. No wonder he sent me to Puerto Rico.

The move to Puerto Rico was hard on me. First it was a place that reminded me of betrayal. Secondly, it pushed me further into feeling alone. There was no healthy outlet for me to vent my frustrations. Imagine sitting in your room, listening to your favorite hip hop album. You're homesick, alone, and feeling betrayed by the people who are supposed to love you the most. You feel like a part of you is lost as you are thinking of home, missing your friends, reminiscing the memories of just kicking with your boys, and many other things. Instead, you are in a place that doesn't feel like home, with no friends, and no one to hang out with. How would you feel in that situation? Probably not the greatest! So, now can you imagine why I had these pent-up emotions? It was rough. On top of all that, it seemed as if no one understood what I was going through. So, when I misbehaved, no one ever asked me what stemmed my behavior. Instead, they asked me to change my behavior. Oh, if it was just that simple!

In school, reputation is typically everything. So, imagine the hit I took, when I had to ride in the back of a truck like some pig being delivered to a farm. Then, jumping out of the truck in front of the school, while everyone is giving you stares. The chuckles that I got, when this gringo, didn't even have a proper ride to school! It was embarrassing. But, I was determined to not allow this setback to define who I was going to be.

In time, my new life in Puerto Rico soon became consumed with days of skipping school, getting low grades, drinking, smoking cigarettes and weed as well. Believe it or not, this foolish behavior was considered completely normal for the average 15-year-old kid there. Having a few beers at the bar and playing a round of pool was the equivalent of what would be, to most of us, grabbing a large popcorn and watching the latest action movie. I was never *peer pressured* into this new lifestyle. All I wanted to do was have a good time and be in the in-crowd, and that's what the in-crowd did. So, I figured, *Why be miserable? Might as well make the best of this situation!*

When I wasn't skipping school, I was there to be the class clown. All that reading and writing stuff wasn't for me. My goal was to be known and be popular. One of the ways I did that was by being the class clown. I had a bag full of taunts, jokes, and smart comments. No one was exempt from being a target of mine, not even teachers.

During one Geometry class, the students sitting in my row were goofing around and causing a lot of noise. Usually, I was the one in the center of all the clowning, but this time, it wasn't me. My teacher, Mrs. Acosta thought differently. Mrs. Acosta irritated, yelled at the class, then specifically calls out my name followed by, "Cut it out!"

In which I reply, "That wasn't me!" By now, all sets of eyes in that classroom were locked in on me.

"Um, yeah, it was you. It always is. So, I suggest you knock it off!" Mrs. Acosta insisted and then proceeded to finish writing the Pythagorean Theorem (this detail is for all the geeks that paid attention in school) on the board. With her back facing the class again, the commotion in my row resumed. Hearing the rustling behind her, Mrs. Acosta whipped her head around and with a snappy high-pitched voice exclaims, "Lo, how many times do I have to keep telling you? Cut it out!" At this point, I had my fill of her blaming me for the incident, so, I retaliated in a way that I felt the situation called for.

"Don't get mad at me because you're going through some personal problems," and then I proceeded to air out her dirty laundry for the whole class to hear. Soon everyone in that room knew about my teacher's divorce and numerous other personal stories. To no one's surprise, Mrs. Acosta cancelled the remainder of class and sent me to the principal's office.

In tears, she gave the principal an ultimatum, "Suspend that kid. Kick him out of school. Do something, or... I quit!" Hearing her words was a shock to my ears. For the first time, I discovered that words have great power. My words were so potent, they almost made my teacher quit her job. As for me, fortunately grace was applied, and I was only suspended for a few days.

However, Mrs. Acosta did have the last laugh. For, she failed me for the school year when I was only 1% away from receiving a passing grade. It hurt, especially when it meant that I had to enroll in summer school.

My mom was probably the reason I got suspended that day instead of expelled. Mom had a magic to her. Perhaps it was her reasoning skills, strong religious convictions, sweet ways, kind demeanor, or fervent prayers. Whatever it was, she succeeded in talking administration out of it. Countless other times, I was threatened to be kicked out of school, and yet, thanks to my mom, I wasn't. Mom was a saint. I know I tested her patience, yet, through it all, her love was consistent and evident. I owe my mom a great debt for defending me numerous times and earning me grace when I least deserved it.

Even though my mom had superpowers, she too reached her breaking point with me. My antics continued to spiral out of control to the point where it got so out of hand, that even patient mom eventually called the cops on me. However, this did not deter me. The rule breaking, sneaking out of the house, skipping school, and drinking continued to escalate. Car robbery even got added on to my rap sheet. My behavior got so terrible that I was threatened with being sent to boot camp.

Fortunately, I discovered one escape from this hell of misconducts–basketball. My love for the game began when I first saw Michael Jordan play. As a kid, I watched with admiration as he hit six 3-pointers in the first half of the 1992 Finals and followed up with that famous shoulder shrug over Clifford Robinson.

My dad and others often shared a bunch of stories about Morovis' hometown team, the Titanes de Morovis, winning the championship in 1985. These stories were inspiring, and I never got tired of listening to them. Naturally, one of my favorite weekend activities became attending these hometown games. Sitting in the bleachers watching the players in action was a dope experience. It was as if I could see myself being on the same court with them. Through the Titanes, I had finally found my dream. I knew what I wanted, and that was to play for the Titanes de Morovis.

Basketball soon became my outlet of escape from everything hurtful in my life. It was the one thing that kept me motivated and helped me find a glimmer of peace during my adjustment to living in Puerto Rico. In the past, I had struggled with prioritizing important things and earning good grades. Thanks to my newfound love of basketball, I managed to maintain high enough grades to keep me eligible to play at school. At least, most of the time that is. There was this one time that I was failing science right before a big tournament. The teacher gave me a passing grade just so I could play. I always figured out how to do just enough to get by, simply so I could play.

As a basketball player, I may not have been the biggest, fastest, or best, but I could always hold my own. The one thing I did have was a jump shot. This is what earned my keep on the basketball court. That jump shot allowed me to experience the island like I never did before.

Thanks to my jumper, doors flung open for me to participate in tournaments and gain the respect of my classmates and teammates. One day, an opportunity came to play for the selection team for Puerto Rico. This was the chance I was looking for. I had the opportunity to play with the top players in my age bracket and compete against other countries. Thanks to basketball, possibilities were made available that I thought were impossible.

Basketball, though a faithful escape route, was not the perfect solution for my problems.

There were few opportunities for me to train, and on top of that, my friends didn't share my love for the game. So, I was left with these blank open spaces of time when I was either wanting to train but couldn't, or, wishing for friends to play with, but couldn't find them. So, during those moments, I chose to skip school, drink, smoke and stay up late roaming the streets instead of working on my game.

My three years in Puerto Rico were awful. However, I

cannot imagine how much worse they were for my poor mother. Amazingly, no matter how many headaches I gave her, moments I irritated her, or the magnitude of misery I contributed to her life, she continually showed me grace and love. Anger and hurt blinded my eyes from seeing her unconditional sacrifice. Instead, revenge consumed me.

One afternoon, my mom took me shopping as a back-to-school gift. It was a thoughtful gesture done out of genuine love. Most teens would hug their mom and say "thank you" as a sign of gratitude. But no, not me. Instead, what did I do for my mom, who had just bought me new clothes with her hard-earned money? I went out and got drunk. What happened to the brand-new clothes? I threw up on them. Right in front of her. To this day, my mom's expression of sadness is smeared into my mind so vividly. She must have wondered if she failed as a mother or questioned if she could have done more. The truth is, she did everything, and there isn't anything more that she could have done. My actions were all my choice. I knew what I was doing, and I wasn't planning to change.

I never envisioned my life to be such a mess, but I just felt so uncared for and deeply hurt. A few close family friends were observant enough to notice my struggles and attempted to reach out to me. They tried to encourage me, help me think about the consequences of my actions, and motivate me to reroute my life. Their efforts were in vain, for their words fell on to deaf ears. I was determined to remain bitter and hate my experience in Puerto Rico. Rebellion was my course, pride was the path I treaded on, and nothing was going to stop me from changing. Until, I heard the following words, which grabbed my attention like nothing else:

"Son, if you behave well enough, I'll let you move back to Orlando," and that's all I needed to hear for me to get my act together.

Often, people do not realize the blessings that surround them until an experience is over. I am one of those people. Unfortunately, it took me years of reminiscing for me to realize that Puerto Rico could have been a better place for me. There were blessings there, but I chose to not receive most of them.

If it weren't for Puerto Rico, I would never have learned to read and write in Spanish (I actually had a better grade in Spanish than in English. True story.) With this acquired language, I am now forever at a greater advantage than many others, thanks again to Puerto Rico. However, aside from that, it's a shame that I never took the time to enjoy the friends and family who surrounded me. We had game nights, celebrated birthdays, and enjoyed laughing at jokes. I could have had more cherished family moments, but instead, I busied myself doing meaningless things like smoking weed and drinking liquor. For three years I was surrounded by gorgeous beaches and mountain views, yet, never stopped to enjoy the beauty that was Puerto Rico. It was a simple life I was forced to live with its absence of television and other flashy distractions. These things created the opportunity for me to capitalize on my goals and dreams. I had the time to do something big, but I never seized the opportunity.

Instead of pleasant emotions being linked with Puerto Rico, rather, the feelings of hurt, anger and betrayal are my memories. Instead of looking inwardly for reasons why I was sent to Puerto Rico and owning up to my mistakes, I pointed my finger at everyone else blaming them for my miseries. Despite all this, people still saw potential in me, but I never lived up to it. Rather, I chose to play the victim. I chose to dwell in my miseries rather than seeking ways to improve my circumstances. Because of that, my negativity caused my situation to get worse. As a result, I hurt myself and others. I made no one proud. There was only disappointment

Often times I wonder, what would it have been like if I had made different choices? How would things have changed if I chose to believe in my potential, if I made a conscious decision to focus on the blessings rather than my failures? What if I had chosen to run every day, go to the basketball court, and take jumpers instead of smoking and drinking? What would it have been like if I used my influence to inspire others instead of tearing them down? Would things have turned out differently if I had just maintained a positive attitude instead of a negative one? There are many questions I don't have answers for. I do know that my poor choices led to adverse consequences, instead of character and personal growth.

There is a saying that goes, "When life hands out lemons, make lemonade." I definitely did not make that my life motto.

What challenges have you faced? Perhaps it is moving to a new state or transferring to a new school? Maybe it is having a child out of wedlock and dealing with the father who has lost his love for you. Is it losing a job, getting cheated on, or failing to be accepted into college? Were you dealt a bad hand? Or, does life plain out suck? No matter the situation, keep in mind that your response to today's challenges determines where you will be and who you will become tomorrow.

From my experience, when a situation may seem bleak, it is very easy to place blame on others for your misfortunes. If you find yourself playing this blame game, here is an acronym that may help: STAR. A good way to remember this is to keep in mind that when the situation is the darkest, as a STAR, you can shine the brightest. STAR stands for the following: **S**TOP, **T**HINK, **A**SK, **R**EFLECT

- **S**top blaming.
- **T**hink about the consequences.
- **A**sk yourself these questions: Will my negative thoughts and actions cause me to make positive choices? Will this decision help make me a better person? Are my actions in line with who I am? Will my actions help me be the person I want to be?
- **R**eflect on the situation.

If only I had challenged myself back in Puerto Rico to stop, think, act, and reflect, perhaps I wouldn't have ended up so angry. Tough situations can either stunt or encourage growth. The way I reacted when I was younger may have stunted me then, but as I got older, I decided that this was not going to be my permanent condition. Years later, I have learned the following valuable lessons from my Puerto Rico experience. These lessons have greatly influenced the way that I now tackle difficult situations. Challenge yourself to apply the following principles and see what good comes out of it:

- **Always act from principle, never from impulse.** Do what's right because it is right.
- **In moments of anger, practice happiness.** Search for the good things from your situation. Though you may be upset about your circumstances, attempt to find joy instead of focusing on the pain.
- **Focus on positive feelings and thoughts.** Erase negative ones. Right thinking will give you right results. With much practice, this will become a habit.
- **Find your dream and work towards it.** Let your goals determine your choices. Doing this provides you with a focus that will allow you to rise above your circumstances.
- **Remember that shortcuts can hurt.** Don't settle for cheap thrills or quick fixes.
- **Accept new situations as a gift.** You never know what great opportunities actually lie ahead of you. Life has many chapters. A chapter may have a bumpy beginning that surprisingly leads to a promising ending.

Life is all about closing old chapters and beginning new ones. It's about rising above these unpleasant chapters so you can face a brand-new possibility-filled chapter with strength, wisdom, and optimism. Unfortunately for me, because I didn't learn these lessons earlier on, this angry chapter of my life seemed to last forever. Kind of like a never-ending rollercoaster ride.

Remember if "Life can dish it. You can take it. Just focus on your goal and don't lose sight of the prize."

QUESTIONS

- Has your anger, hurt and frustration ever caused you to become somebody you never thought you would become? If so, looking back now, how would you have handled those negative emotions differently?
- Many teenagers are peer pressured into doing drugs and alcohol. Why do you believe those things are used as an outlet to escape difficulties? What other outlets are there? What are yours?
- What differences exist between being raised in a home with both parents present versus a single parent home? List the advantages and disadvantages for both.

CHAPTER 3

THE RETURN

"Who the f*%# spit in this condom? Who wrote in this card and said that they used it on my girl?" yelled this rich kid to one of my boys as we were all hanging out by the guy's dorm during lunch break. It's crazy that this classmate, who we all felt had a silver spoon in his mouth, was trying to come hard at us. For a rich white kid, he sure was ticked off. He leaned over my boy, clenching his fists, ready to throw a punch, "Admit it, you did it b%&*!"

As we all stood there watching this argument unfold. I realized something was going to pop off. My boy was upset that the rich white kid was all in his face. So, my boy got up and got in the rich white kid's face. Tensions were growing, and we all could feel it.

"I'm not going to say it again....Who the f*&$ did this?" the rich white kid questioned angrily.

"And if I don't?" replied my boy. That response ticked the rich white kid off, and boom! Just like that, he threw a fist. In an instant, there was a full outright brawl between myself and some of my friends. Shoving, punching, headlocks, and curse words. Everything happened so fast! The fight grew so large, that bystanders even jumped in to try to break it up.

I already had a reputation for being a troublemaker, but I definitely didn't want to get in trouble for fighting. So, when things cooled down a bit, I quickly fled the scene and took off to the student lounge. My adrenaline was still pumping, but I was glad the fight was all over.

Word of the fight had already gotten around by the time I reached the student lounge. When I got there, I was still so pumped up from the fight, that I continued telling people around me about it. Then, all of a sudden, I saw the door to the student center fling open. I looked towards the door, and there I saw, storming in, was the dude I got into a fight with. My adrenaline was still pumping. Clearly, I still wasn't over the fight and was still pissed. As I saw him, I told myself, *You got to be kidding me?* Anything at that point would have pushed me over the top, so it didn't help when he opened up his mouth. All I knew was that I wanted to bust this dude's head.

I got up from the bench to approach him, wanting to give him a piece of my mind. But fortunately for him, the science teacher walked by and grabbed me by the shirt before I could actually do anything. "Woah, Lo you need to calm down and go that way!" he said, pointing to the exit door. "Leave the student center, now!" I obeyed, but as I was leaving, the dude kept yelling stuff at me which got me even more agitated.

I then heard a familiar voice, "Loammi, go straight to the principal's office."

Without a second thought, I shouted back, "I ain't goin' to no mother (you fill in the blank) office." That was the last straw. I should have taken a few seconds to think about what I was saying and realize who I was talking to because it was no one else but the principal! My dream of attending Forest Lake Academy came to a close.

Before this all happened, I thought my wish had come true. I was back in Orlando. My friends and I were excited about attending this new school, and I knew that it was going to be a dope school year. I had two main goals for that year. My first goal was to be the popular kid in school. My second goal involved some hoop dreams of making the varsity team. The next three years of high school were going to be the best times of my life. That was the plan. That was the dream. But it was all short lived.

The day I got into the fight my parents were called in for a parent-teacher conference. By the time the conference ended, I knew those dreams were gone. Angry, frustrated and disappointed, I walked through Forest Lake Academy's double glass doors one last time. Ugh, *how did I just manage to get myself kicked out? I had big plans!*

I had just sabotaged my own high school dreams. No more varsity team. Peace out to the homies. And popularity? Well, I gained that, but all for the wrong reasons. The fight may have earned me some sort of rep, but that wasn't the kind I was looking for. The moment I jumped into that brawl I basically kissed my high school dreams goodbye.

If I were to be fair and honest with myself, I would have kicked myself out of school too. My GPA was horrible, and because of my family's financial situation, I paid next to nothing to attend. I was more of a head case than an asset to the school. The teachers thought I was not going to amount to anything. I am sure they were glad to kick me out.

After all that happened, the drama from Puerto Rico began haunting me all over again. My thoughts spiraled. *How could this be? Orlando was supposed to be better. It wasn't supposed to be this way!* It's as if I was stuck on this ongoing rollercoaster. It seemed as if I was just going in cycles.

Why was I going through these cycles? Many reasons.

There were lessons I should have learned from Puerto Rico, but never did.

My past issues were not resolved, just masked.

I never learned how to control my mouth or my attitude, nor did I learn from any of my other mistakes.

It may have seemed like I had improved my behavior towards the end of my stay in Puerto Rico, but that was just because I wanted to convince my parents to allow me to return to Orlando. The sad reality is that I enjoyed my bad habits and poor choices such as drinking, smoking, and skipping class. Even the disappointment in my mom's eyes when she saw me slumped over drunk was not enough to make me quit drinking.

As a saying goes, old habits are hard to break. Though I was back home, where I wanted to be, I still wasn't a new me. Unfortunately, I had returned to my default habits of skipping classes, disruptive behavior, and frequent visits to the principal's office. Plus, I had just added *involved in one of the largest fights in school* to the list.

For the first time, thanks to getting kicked out of Forest Lake Academy, I experienced suffering the consequences of my actions. I felt it hard. The fight landed me at Maynard Evans High, one of the worst schools in the county. The other high schools that were in my district, Apopka and Edgewater High, would have been more appealing options. But no, my luck landed me with what I thought was the *garbage school*. There were so many rumors about Evans High School. A lady once told me a crazy story about a student stabbing another with an HIV needle. (Later, I did discover that these rumors were far from the truth.)

For my entire life, I had always attended private schools. Because of this, I knew that Evans High was going to be a life-changing experience. I didn't know how I was going to handle being out of my private-school bubble. My mind flooded with nervous questions. *How was public school going to work? Would I fit in? What were the teachers going to be like? For sure it was going to be a whole new adventure, filled with possible fights, scares of HIV and all. Was I mentally prepared for what I was about to enter?*

The first day of school at Evans High arrived. That morning, I stood on a street corner waiting for the school bus to pull up. It was still dark. The weather was a little nippy, and I was anxiously waiting to see how my first day in public school was going to be. Once I got off the bus, I quickly realized how big the school was. Forest Lake Academy had around 500 students, and this new school had about 5,000. Maynard Evans was massive. There were so many students and so much ruckus in the hallways. It was like entering into a new world. There were long hallways with rows of lockers. There were students with dread heads, cornrows, taper fades, weaves, Baby Fat clothing, Girbaud jeans, you name it.

I stared, taking it all in. Everyone was so loud. Many looked rough, and some looked straight up scary. There were real athletes at this school too, not just *wanna be's* like at my old school. *So, this is it!* I knew I had to act cool, as if I had been in this situation before. However, my insecurities quickly kicked in. At my old school, I was known as being the loud, funny, troublemaker, but now I realized that everyone was this person too. *Who would I be? How would I fit in?* I was back to square one, wondering....*Who am I?*

In order for me to adjust to this new setting, I knew I needed to do something to stand out. At all my previous schools, I was the class clown. I wasn't just *a* class clown; I was *the* class clown. That's what made me popular. So, now being in public school, everyone had my same title. I knew I had to push the limits to be recognized. And that's exactly what I did.

One day, in science class, one of the students tried to clown me. In the middle of class, he came across the room and bumped my chair. No apologies. Nothing. To make matters worse, he put his butt all in my face. Frustrated, because I didn't know what to do, I knew I had to figure out something quick.

There was no way I was going to let this guy try me in front of the class. If he bumped into me again, I knew I had to say something. Like clockwork, he got back up and proceeded to walk to the front of the class and bump me in the process.

"Bruh, this is going to be the last time you bump into me. And, I suggest, you get yo a#$ out of my face!" I exclaimed.

He turned, looked me in the eye, and answered, "Naw, you straight? If I'm in your way, then you move."

"Well, if you don't move outta the way, then I'll make you move." I threatened.

At this point the entire class was locked into the back and forth. Everyone was watching and wondering what the new kid was going to do.

"Just as I thought, you ain't going to do *$&#*%&!" he

taunted and turned to leave. It only took a split second for him to return and piss me off all over again with the same butt-in-my-face routine. I knew I was getting clowned. I had to think and do something ASAP.

"Since you like puttin' yo behind in men's faces...." I stated as I took the pencil I had in hand and shoved it up his _____. Well, there's only one place I could shove it. I gave Buddy a straight up enema.

All I heard from the class was, "Ooooooh snap," as they all went crazy. Buddy's eyes bogged out of his head. I have never seen anyone so mad in my life. Luckily the science teacher intervened before a fight broke out right there and then.

"You *$&#$@! I'm gonna knock your a@# out after class!" Buddy was clearly pissed about what just happened. I'd be lying if I didn't tell you that I was a little nervous too. All my life I did a lot of trash talking but little fighting. However, there was no way I was going to be intimidated by this situation. I had to stand my ground, and I wasn't going to get bullied or punked. Not today.

The bell rang. Class was dismissed. It was a crazy scene. Students were rushing to the cafe, flooding from all directions, yelling and telling everyone that a fight was about to go down. I had to swim through this chaos just to make it there myself. I looked around and didn't see Buddy. Instead, I found a group of people that I knew, and hung out with them while hoping this would all blow over. Eventually, the ole boy did find me.

"So you think you funny?!" Buddy yelled.

I replied back, "Naw, ain't nobody funny. Only funny dude is you, sticking yo butt in people's faces."

By now, it felt like the whole school was gathered around ready to witness our fight. I was pissed. I talked my smack; he talked his. I was waiting for him to take the first swing because I didn't want to be the one who *started the fight*. Eventually, I got the best of him as he was clearly also too scared to throw the first punch. Probably for the same reason why I didn't throw mine. Thankfully nothing more happened.

The *fight* was a pivotal moment in my public school experience. I did walk away that day earning the respect from a lot of my peers and even from the dude who wanted to fight. The school year continued, and Evans High began to grow on me. I ended up loving it there. I developed some strong friendships (that I have kept to this very day), and for the first time in a long time, I felt like I fit in. At Evans High, I learned so much about the Black culture because it was predominantly a Black high school. I was learning so much about myself, who I was, and who I was becoming. I loved my school and my new friends. I felt as if I had finally found a home– somewhere I felt I belonged.

Surprisingly, my grades also actually started to improve. The operative word from the previous sentence is *improve*. Though my grades were improving (which was an accomplishment on its own), they were still not good enough to allow me to try out for the basketball team. Unfortunately, I didn't get my GPA up until my final semester of my senior year. Looking back, I think I had a chance to make at least the JV team. There was a lot of talent at Evans High. In 2002, we were ranked Number 1 in state and Top 25 in the country. Orlando was booming with talent at that time. Players like Amare Stoudumire, Darius Washington, Marquis Daniel, Yusuf Baker, Cartlon Christian and Brandon Siler were all local players. All these guys either played Division 1 basketball, went on to play in the NBA, or the NFL. Even though I wasn't on the team, I was friends with most of the guys on the team. I was there for every big rival game, getting hyped with all my boys. Friday night games were the place to be on the weekends. These games were the one time where I could fully be me.

Evans High ended up having more positives than I anticipated. I was improving my behavior (somewhat), grades were going up, and as mentioned before, I was getting accustomed to fitting into my new school. Unfortunately, my mouth did get me into trouble a lot, and I landed several times in in-school suspension because I could never keep my mouth shut. Also, I couldn't seem to fully let go of many of the habits I had picked up in Puerto Rico.

I still loved drinking and that continued every Friday of my senior year. Every Friday morning, one of my homies would go across the street to the Winn Dixie supermarket and steal a bottle of liquor. Before coming to school, we would go to McDonald's, order breakfast, and fill our cups with either Fruitopia or Twister drinks. We'd sip on that cup all day long (if y'all don't know about those drinks, then you missed out. Man, I miss high school.). Every Friday, we got lit during school.

In addition to drinking, fights were still a thing for me because I still had this chip on my shoulder. People always seemed to test me because I was light skinned, or the *pretty boy*, making them think I was soft. This was something that I always had to deal with. A lot of this testing occurred at the Caribbean Beach Club, one of the spots my friends and I would go to on the weekends. This spot was well known for the reggae room, hip-hop, and all the fights that would occur every Saturday night. Countless times, I was the star of these fights because either I was the one starting it or just involved in the heat of it all. This is what my boys and I did for entertainment. Yeah, it was reckless, but this is the mischief we would get into. We would always return with these wild stories of what happened over the weekend. The downside is that all the fighting and beefing did eventually take its toll and cause me to lose a lot of friends and acquaintances. What we thought was innocent and fun ended up causing a lot of hurt and even death. Often the hype of a lifestyle is glorified, but no one ever shows the ugly truth hidden on the other side. For me, this ugly truth was my reality.

I was always down for my boys and pledged a sense of loyalty to them. I'd fight for them. All the time. However, God must have really been looking out for me all those years, because I'd somehow happen to dodge the massive fights that ended with gunshots. It just so happened, that during the nights where guns were involved, I was not around. Something would happen, either I got kicked out before it all occurred, or I came to the club too late for the action. My guardian angel found creative means like these to keep me away from the greater danger.

All this fighting eventually caught up with me. One Saturday night, my boys from the football and basketball team were hanging out at Universal City Walk. This was where we frequently went on Saturday nights to hang out, catch the latest movie, or grab a bite to eat. On this particular evening, one of my homie's little brother and his group of boys got into an altercation with some people. These kids were young, around 12-13 years old. Curious to see what was happening, we all walked over to the group of young boys, and also attempted to break up the fight. One of the bystanders, seeing the group of guys just double in size, called security and told them that the 6'6" black guy in the middle of the pack, named Kadeem, was responsible for the fight. The thing was, Kadeem was actually trying to help break up the fight, not the one responsible for it! He was trying to help! And so was I. It so happened that the little brother we were trying to help was white, and security pegged the black dude instead.

In no time, the Universal City Walk Security had Kadeem surrounded. It was obvious that security too pegged him as the main culprit, and they flooded him with questions. It was like a rapid-fire sequence of questions, clearly pinning him as the guilty party and instigator of the fight. Kadeem kept trying to tell security the truth. However, at this point, security was acting in mob mentality. They had the wrong guy! Security wasn't hearing anything that Kadeem had to say. They already had their minds made up. Kadeem was frustrated. You could see it in his face. Kadeem's situation was heating up, and the guards even threatened him with pepper spray. Of course, my boy Kadeem was pissed.

I couldn't stand there watching Kadeem go down for something he didn't do. So, I sprinted over in his direction and yelled, "Yo, he isn't the one!" As I was running towards the chaos, trying to diffuse the situation, I felt a firm hand grab me from behind. As my natural reflexes go, I stiffed up my arm, turned around, and threw a punch without even looking to see who was behind me. Just my luck. I threw that punch to a police officer.

My adrenaline was pumping so high, it took about eight security guards and a police officer to take me down to the ground. Soon, I found myself in handcuffs and detained in a security room.

After some questioning, the officer that arrested both of us realized we weren't bad guys or teens out causing trouble. Fortunately, the night had somewhat of a silver lining because the officer actually ended up taking a liking to us once he got to understand the situation and know all of us better. After we cooled down, we quickly realized the amount of trouble we'd just gotten into. Lucky for me, the officer dropped my charge from *resisting arrest with violence* to *resisting arrest without violence*. The initial charge carried a more severe punishment than the one I ended up being given. This was a blessing because I probably deserved a tougher punishment since this was not my first arrest as a juvenile.

Once again, I was off to Juve. But this time it was different, I was asked the following question: Were you ever arrested before? My thoughts raced. *Ummm...what do I say? Do I tell them the truth and look like a repeat offender? Or, do I lie and save face?*

"Nope, never been to Juve," I lied. The officer called my bluff pretty quickly after booking my name and pulling up my past arrest record. I was detained for the night. The following morning, the overseeing officer decided to release me. He placed a call to my mom and told her to pick me up. She refused. The officer then called my dad, who also refused to pick me up. Both of my parents actually agreed on not picking me up. Instead, they left me there to process everything right there with servings of cold sandwiches, in an uncomfortable cell, and with constant interrogation about crimes that I had not committed. Apparently, constant interrogation has worked in the past. Some people actually crack and end up confessing under pressure.

While there, some intern (can't remember his name) kept befriending me and continued asking me various questions about my arrest and what happened to me that night. He was a dude no older than 30 and he tried to get information that could incriminate me. I kept telling the intern that I had no clue what he was talking about. He later found out that the questions he was asking were being asked to the wrong person. He thought I was involved with some fight that involved a gun. He later explained how kids would brag about what they did just to later find themselves in trouble for sharing too much information. It was all together a crazy night.

The torture of this evening lasted longer than I felt it needed to. My parents never came to pick me up until the weekend was over. I could have come home, but my parents chose to leave me in Juve. Yes, they allowed their own son to be locked up at their own free will. I later learned that they were fed up with me, and this was their way showing tough love because they didn't know what else to do.

That weekend in the juvenile detention center felt like a month. I was drowning in self-incriminating thoughts and weighing my value in life. Anxious for the moment my parents would pick me up, I started to wonder, *How did I get here? I know I always put myself in these situations, but this wasn't my fault. I tried doing the right thing. Why can't I just do right? This ain't me!*

Sometime after being picked up from Juve, I discovered that due to being a repeat offender, I had to face the judge and plead my case. I didn't know what to do. I had never had to face a judge before. *How would I plead my case? What would I say?* So, I sought advice from the people that loved me the most–my parents.

My parents each gave me their two cents. They gave me conflicting advice, leaving me even more confused. My dad told me to plead *no contest*. My mother, on the other hand, suggested that I plead *guilty*. Yes, guilty. My own mother told me to plead guilty. She had her reasons, but, regardless, I couldn't believe it.

The day finally arrived when I had to face the judge. It felt like an eternity before my name was called. My stomach was filled with butterflies. My nerves were shot and all I could do was shake my leg nervously waiting for my name to be called. I listened nervously to all the sentences that were handed out before me. Some of the cases, many of them were crazy to hear, and a lot of them involved serving time. I wasn't ready for all that. I wasn't really this tough guy that I was portraying to be. I had heard enough stories of what happens in Juve. I was shook. Inside, I was falling apart.

Finally, after the long agonizing wait, I heard the Judge's firm voice state my name with commanding force, "Lo-Ammi Richardson." My turn had come. I had to face whatever my sentence was. I had to plead my case. My parents accompanied me to the front where I stood before the judge. I was scared as hell.

The judge began by reading my charges. My heart was beating out of my chest. My imagination was racing with crazy scenarios. I still didn't know what to do. I felt as if my life and my future were hanging there in the balance.

After what felt like an eternity, I heard the judge ask the dreaded question, "Lo-Ammi, what do you plead?" Still unsure of my response, I gave my mom a side glance just in time to see her nod at me. I knew what she meant with the nod. Plea G-U-I-L-T-Y! I was reluctant but complied to her advice.

With all the courage I could scrape up, I muttered the words that I knew would only incriminate my own self, "Guilty. I plead guilty." The judge was taken back by my response. It was obvious by the stunned look he had plastered all over his face. Everyone before me had pleaded not guilty for their charges, except for me. "Sir, I am guilty for my actions, but not for the reason I got in trouble. You see, I was helping a friend. I was trying to help him not get into trouble, but in the process of helping him, my temper and actions got in the way. Obviously, my temper and my actions is what led me to be standing here." It was hard for me to read what the judge thought of my response, but he seemed astonished and possibly even slightly impressed. I don't think it was what he was expecting. The room was silent. The judge then transferred his attention to my parents and asked them if there was anything they wanted to say.

What happened during the next few moments was nothing short of amazing. My mom spoke up, and the words flowing from her mouth were like honey, as if inspired by God himself. "Sir, I have something I want to say," acknowledging her opportunity to speak, "I see on your name plate that you are Judge Rodriguez. Rodriguez is a special name, for before I got married, I was also a Rodriguez."

I glanced over at my mom, wondering, *Mom, where are you going with this?* But there was no stopping her.

My mom then pointed to a seal that was placed behind his seat. "You see, sir, we should trust in God. God sets up judges and raises them. You, sir, were called by God to be a judge over these teenagers and the responsibilities he holds over the youth to make better decisions. My son is guilty, and he is willing to take any punishment you give him. (Can you imagine the look I shot my mom with when she ended that mini sermon of hers? I was horrified.)

My mom's soliloquy left the judge momentarily speechless. In that split moment of silence, the judge made his decision on my case. He banged his gavel and then announced my sentence. Probation. Only probation. It was clear that the judge was impressed by my mom's words. He contributed that probation was my punishment, instead of something worse, because he saw that my mother was a Godly woman. Once again, my mom had come to my rescue. My eyes were opened to my reality. It clicked. I didn't realize how much my parents cared for me until I was in the most trouble. The judge also suggested that I take anger management classes since I clearly had issues in this area. I knew if I complied it would lower my sentence.

Probation sucked. Being stuck at home and having a curfew really put a damper on things for me. My dad did use my probation against me a lot of the times. From my perspective, he used it as a tool to try to establish some ground rules that he knew couldn't be implemented if it weren't for my probation. I didn't always obey the rules of my probation. I can recount multiple times I stayed out late doing stuff I wasn't supposed to do. However, being on probation definitely made me more cautious of the decisions I was making.

After probation ended, I decided to finally get my act together for graduation was around the corner. I turned over some new leaves and tried my best to be a "good kid", and not a juve one. I was determined to not be a high school dropout because I wanted to graduate. I wanted to accomplish something that my parents didn't get to accomplish and didn't want to be a further embarrassment to myself or them. So, I worked hard and tried to stay out of trouble. I strived to pass the standardized testing for graduation, and I did it! My final GPA was boosted to a 2.4, and I even managed to complete high school with 16 extra credits. Despite all the setbacks and mistakes I had made, I was still able to accomplish a big goal in my life, to graduate high school. I, Lo-Ammi Richardson, was a high school graduate! This was a great feat and major accomplishment for me. Many of my friends never graduated high school. To this day, some still don't even have their GED.

The day finally arrived that I had been dreaming about for quite some time. I wanted that diploma so badly, and there was nothing that was going to stop me from walking across that stage to receive it in my hand. That diploma was like a golden ticket for me, a golden ticket that would prove that I am not a failure. A golden ticket that proves that with hard work and focus you can accomplish things. When my name was called, and I stretched out my hand to receive it, my heart filled with pride. This diploma was a symbol to me that I could begin putting my mistakes as a juve behind me. I could finally put all that ugliness into the past and start a new beginning. I was determined to learn from my mistakes and grow from my experiences.

Just like the return of Lebron to Cleveland, my time had its up and it's down. I finally settled into what I wanted to become. I had roots now, and I felt like I had to put the city on my back. As I reflect and think about my time in high school, I realize that a lot of the issues I had came from not having someone to reach out to and talk to about my problems. I had anger issues, and because of that anger, I made choices and mistakes that affected my outlook on life. I never had anyone to talk to or someone I could confide in. There was no one to point out the things I was doing wrong.

Additionally, I never liked to talk about my problems until I got into trouble. It was a cycle that I needed to break out of, and I quickly realized I didn't know how to break out of it. I held a lot of emotions and pain inside. One thing I learned while taking my anger management sessions was not to hold those negative thoughts or feelings inside too long. I learned that we need to vent them out to someone we know and trust. If not, then those feelings eventually grow and become bigger issues, which can then cause us to respond in a negative way.

Remember that every action repeated forms a habit. Habits formulate your character, and your character determines what destiny you will choose. Little did I know that my actions were developing a character that didn't align with what I was created and designed to be.

If you are struggling with pain, anger or identity, ask yourself, *What do you want to be? Who do you want to become? What do you want people to remember you as?* Next, think about the choices you are making. Are the choices you are making creating a character that reflects the person you want to be? What habits are you creating for yourself? Are they good or are they bad? I never understood this point until after seeing all the setbacks I was experiencing because of the choices I was making. I didn't take well to authority. Why? Because I didn't know who I was, and because of that I allowed the environment I was in to dictate what I thought I should be. All this stemmed from pain I didn't know I still had. Because of that pain, it led me to continue to express that pain by getting into fights, drinking, and making questionable decisions. This behavior set me back in high school. Maybe I could have played Varsity basketball, who knows. What I know is that if I kept the big picture in mind, dealt with the issues I had, then things would have gone a lot different.

QUESTIONS

- Have there been moments in your life that you wished you were dealt a different hand? If so, what would be different?
- Reflect on your childhood, was there a pivotal moment that defined you? Whether good or bad? How did you respond to that moment? How has it affected you now?
- What differences do youth, raised in two-parent homes, versus single parent homes experience? List the pros and cons for each type of home.
- Will the choices you make now affect you in the future? Explain your answer.

CHAPTER 4

SELECTION DAY

The biggest day for any student athlete is Selection Day. This is the day that all top athletes from around the country choose which University they will play for and commit their talents to. There have been many high school student athletes who have gone on to college and have had very successful professional and athletic careers.

Every student athlete feels the pressure and nerves on Selection Day, when they finally have to make a decision on which college they will attend. Sometimes there's outside pressure from scouts, boosters and coaches. Not to mention, family and friends can add to that stress when they drop hints of their own college suggestions. However, when it's all said and done, the decision still lies solely between the student and their heart's desire.

Hearts race and pound as media, local newspapers, friends, family and classmates all await the big decision. This is exactly how I felt after my high school graduation. I may not have been a student athlete, but for me, I had a Selection Day. My Selection Day was having to make my big college decision. Do I attend college locally? Or, do I move to another city and attend college there instead?

At first, I decided to attend the local community college. However, after a year of studying in Orlando, I decided that it was time for a change. Student athletes often change their minds too. Sometimes their initial choice doesn't end up working out, so they too may transfer. This is in fact what I did. I transferred. One day, the opportunity to transfer to Tampa Bay popped up. Without hesitation, I took the opportunity and moved my talents down I-4 West on to Tampa, FL.

Once student athletes decide on their college route, their next decision is to declare a course to pursue. I too had to do the same, except I had a dilemma. I couldn't decide on a major. To be completely honest, I didn't really care for school in the first place. I barely graduated from high school and felt that pursuing a higher education was not that important. However, all my friends were doing the college thing, so I decided to jump in on that same bandwagon.

My transfer led me to Hillsborough Community College down in Tampa with no real sense of direction. One thing I knew was that I still had hoop dreams I wanted to pursue. In high school, I lost my opportunity to play because of my poor grades and other bad choices I made. After high school graduation, I did attend a few tryouts for some of the local Community Colleges in the state with some of my boys from the Varsity team at Evans. However, trying out for teams without any highlight tapes, conversations with coaches, and even experience in camps or AAU teams was difficult because I had to create some hype for myself. I needed to compensate for what I was lacking just so I could have real opportunity. Without the decorated list of prior hoop experiences, I realized that my dream of playing college ball was going to be hard to fulfill. My past choices were clearly affecting my current situation and potential dreams. The situation could have been different, but I had to play the cards that were handed to me. This was a reminder that the mistakes one makes in the past can affect the dreams of our future.

This realization of the past affecting my current opportunities became very clear one memorable day. Before making the move to Tampa, a bunch of my boys from my senior year of high school, who were once on the Varsity Team, had a few tryouts lined up. I asked if it was cool for me to join them. Without hesitation they invited me along. Excitedly, I jumped into the SUV and off we went to the tryouts. The community college where tryouts were held was a few hours away from Orlando. I wasn't supposed to be there. I wasn't invited by the college to come. It was a player only invite, and I wasn't a Varsity player. The basketball coach from Evans spoke to the coach of the community college and told him about some players that he should check out.

After a two-hour ride, we finally arrived to our destination. I jumped out the car and felt the sun beaming on my face. Nerves and excitement ran through my bones as I stepped foot into the gym with the boys. We introduced ourselves to the coach who greeted us with a warm welcome and thanked us for coming out. The tryout began with a few drills followed by a scrimmage. My boys and I were then placed on a squad together facing the opposing team, which were the college players themselves! I was nervous and anxious. Even though I wasn't supposed to be there, I figured, if I balled out, it won't matter if I was invited or not.

The ball was inbounded, and the game began. We held our own, but you can tell this college team had great athletes and chemistry, something that I wasn't able to muster with my boys since I never played Varsity with them. One turnover here, a few missed shots later, and before I knew it, the coach asked me what my name was. This was not a good sign. I knew, the name asking, wasn't for any good reason. It was to verify whether or not I was on the team because my play gave away the fact that I had no experience. The next thing I knew I was subbed out and didn't scrimmage for the rest of the day. I wasn't prepared for this opportunity. Therefore, I had a hard time seizing it! It was obvious that my boys' game story was different from mine. The difference between me and them was that they had previous varsity experience. I had zero. This has always lingered in the back of my mind. I wished so badly to have what they had–the experience. What if things were different? What if I did get my act together and took things serious like I was supposed to? Would I have been given a better shot? Who knows, but it's something that I think about quite often. I wonder if my college basketball experience would have been different if I had just strived for good grades and instead focused my energy in trying to be a good student in high school. If only I had paid attention in class and channeled my energy on schoolwork instead of being a class clown. Then, maybe I would have had the opportunity to play ball.

College life was another new world. I quickly learned that high school and college are two very different atmospheres. High school was about the flash, the fashion and the popularity. Having the J's and keeping up with the latest trends mattered. In college, people could care less if your clothing matched or not. High school was a popularity contest, and that's why I had to strive so hard to maintain my class clown status. In college, popularity went down the drain, instead goals, majors, and other priorities took the cake (at least for most people).

Once again, in Tampa, I found myself to be quite lost in this new atmosphere. What I was used to didn't exist. I had no tricks in my pocket and no major to declare. I wanted to play ball, but nothing really panned out for me. Though I attended classes, my grades weren't the best. The only thing that kept me motivated and interested in school to some degree was this pretty check I would receive every semester simply for attending and maintaining a reasonable GPA.

In time, even that money motivator lost its power. I wanted money, but not at the expense of sitting in a classroom all day. Cheap thrills, such as money and popularity, that don as motivators, don't typically have long lasting magic. The motivation eventually dies. College showed me that. I was surrounded by students who were motivated intrinsically to succeed, simply because that was their heart's desire. Not me. My motivation was money, parties, popularity, and all the flash. All this didn't existent in my college experience. These things became my priority because I lacked vision. King Solomon stated that *without a vision the people perish*. This was my story. I was a boy with no purpose. My lack of vision for my life caused me to perish.

Some students choose to transfer to a different college for a new start. I chose to do the same thing. After a year of attending college in Orlando, I transferred so I could take the opportunity to move to Tampa with one of my homies. I thought that this would be a good move for me. I would be able to start a new chapter (again) at a place I wasn't familiar with and a place where nobody knew me. However, it may have been a new place, but sadly, old habits die hard, and I found myself lost and a mess once again. My lack of interest in school resulted in the same outcome. No vision. No drive. No goals.

Not having a sense of direction is a common problem that many seem to experience. People may experience this once in their life and learn to dream and carve a path for themselves. Others, like myself, may find themselves perpetually seeking a need for direction and the right source of motivation.

What are you passionate about? Do you know what you are called to do? If your answer is no, that's okay. Take your time to explore, seek, and find it. Just steer away from what I did. Don't jump on the bandwagon just to feel included. That's the worst thing you can do. You can listen to the suggestions of others but only take them if they align with what's morally astute and foundational to your dreams. Remember, it's your dreams, not theirs.

Everyone is not set for the same path. Education is important, but the type of education you receive is just as vital. College wasn't for me, but I loved basketball. What if I had learned how to train athletes and take the knowledge to help others improve their game? What if I had created content for basketball players to develop certain skills, or developed a class where student athletes could maximize their opportunities? The list for me could have gone on. There are endless possibilities for you. Just choose what you feel like you are called to be.

Set a vision. Set a goal. Keep those two things at the

forefront of your mind. Doing this will keep you on a path that allows you to focus on the big picture. Don't worry about what everyone is doing and what they suggest you should do. Remember it's your Selection Day.

QUESTIONS

- What vision do you have for yourself? What goals do you want to accomplish? What steps will you take to accomplish both of those things?
- Why is it that individuals tend to follow the suggestions of family, friends and society, instead of following what they feel called to do?
- Has the influence of others crippled you from stepping out and making a decision that you wanted to make?
- Is your identity rooted in your vision? If so, explain why or why not?

CHAPTER 5
WHO AM I?

Have you ever asked yourself the question, "Who am I?" Have you ever wondered how you ended up becoming the very thing you said you'll never be? Ever questioned how you ended up in certain not-so-good situations? These were the very questions that I myself have wrestled with multiple times. At the end of the day, I'd find myself looking in the mirror and asking myself this main question, "Who am I?"

At this point in my life, I had become the very person I never wanted to be. The person staring back at me in the mirror, my current self, was not someone that even my wildest imagination could have envisioned. Where did this person come from? How did I get to this point? Simple. By living for myself and nobody else. I was simply doing me and could care less what people thought. There was a world out there that I wanted to conquer, and I was willing to conquer it at the expense of any experience that I might face. My choice of music was my accomplice and greatly influenced my channels of thought and choices of lifestyle. Because of all this, that stranger in the mirror, was in fact, me.

From the outside looking in, one would think I grew up in the mean streets of Chicago or Brooklyn based on how I talked and conducted myself. Those large iconic cities, with their rich history of gang life, weren't my home. Instead, I grew up in a typical middle-class home in Orlando, Florida, in the region of Lockhart, to be exact.

All cities have their version of what we would call the *hood*, and Orlando was no exception. The majority of my time was spent in Orlando's *hood*. It was this place called Pine Hills, otherwise known as *Crime Hills*. I ran around and did *hood* things. I had *hood* friends. In contrast, my home life was nothing like the *hood*. Rather, it was a place of Godly influence free from violence, cursing, or stealing. Hanging out in the hood and doing ratchet activity was entirely my choice.

The way I talked, walked, and thought was something that I learned and mimicked from the crowd I chose to hang with and the music that I listened to. I grew up with a decent structured upbringing, which should have helped me to make better decisions than the ones I was currently making, but I still decided to do things my way.

Living in Tampa was a fresh start for me, a brand-new chapter. I was a stranger in this town. All I wanted to do was play ball, get money, and have a good time. That's why I had chosen to move there.

Tampa became my current home thanks to an invite from one of my good friends, Wayne, who was planning on moving there to finish his degree at the University of South Florida (USF). My boy Wayne and I went as far back as middle school. He was this level headed guy, who had this incredible ability to save money, while simultaneously being able to maximize his resources. I actually looked up to Wayne.

My admiration for him went all the way back to our younger days. That was the first time I noticed and appreciated his hustle. In middle school, when everyone was buying the latest kicks, Wayne would instead be working and saving. He would often include me in his money making ideas. Together we would hustle sodas after school and come home with a good $25-30 bucks. In high school, other dudes and I would always clown him and ask why he would never go out like everyone else. His response was always predictable, "I'm working!"

All his hard work paid off, when one day during a school beach outing, out of nowhere, Wayne pulled up with this car. No one was expecting this. All eyes were following him as he swerved around the corner and parked the car in front of us. Wayne was the first person out of all of us to have a whip. At that point, I got the picture. It was obvious where his head was. Grind now. Ball later.

Dedicated and focused on his hustle, that was Wayne, the dude who managed to turn sodas into a ton of cash and own his first car. So, of course, when Wayne invited me to move up to Tampa with him, I jumped on the opportunity without a bit of hesitation. I knew I couldn't let this chance pass. Living with Wayne would help me move forward. Now was my chance to observe how he saved, worked, and hustled. I wanted the discipline that Wayne had, and I wanted to learn how to bank cash and build for the future.

Once I made the move to Tampa, one of the first things I did was register for school. Though my interest in school wasn't high, I knew that I could easily get a few grand at the end of the semester simply by attending classes. That was motivation enough. I also found a part time job at the YMCA, and eventually landed an additional full-time job at Walmart with Wayne.

In time, I felt as if I was finally settling into my new home and this new chapter in my life. So far, it was a successful chapter for with it came my own independence and the fresh start that I was searching for.

Though I was working two jobs and going to school, I always hustled on the side. As time progressed, I got to meet some new people and made some connections. New friends and new connections meant the start of a vibrant and lively Tampa social life. Soon, I was back to that old familiar norm of clubbing, drinking and smoking.

All throughout my life, I was the connect man. People always contacted me to connect them to something that they needed. If you needed speakers, I knew somebody who had them. It didn't matter what you needed, even if you wanted a suit. I knew a guy who sold them from the back of his truck.

In Tampa, I worked my same game and made new connections. Except this time, I decided to use my connections for myself and reap my own benefits.

Some of my new connections allowed me to get access to weed. This side hustle at first was nothing big, just simple nickel and dime-ing when I needed some extra cash. It was easy for me to sell weed. Simple supply and demand. The people I hung out with smoked, so I provided it for them at a reasonable price. The weed that my connection had was good, and the people who smoked it thought it had good quality. It was such a satisfying feeling to be able to get something and flip it for profit. For example, my homeboy from Orlando would sell a QP (quarter pound) of weed for 75 bucks. The price people would normally pay for that amount would be anywhere from $150-$180 depending on what type of weed it was. No need to break it down. Easy money. For me, it was too much of a hassle to sit there and break down all that weed by ounces and sell them in increments of 5, 10 or even 20-dollar bags. In my opinion, it was a waste of time to do all that work. Though I did it at times, it wasn't my norm. All that meticulous counting, measuring, packaging, and dealing with those small bills drove me nuts. I ditched the small money mindset and decided to go big instead.

Selling weed became my thing. I had found my hustle. It was never my intention to sell drugs, but since I had the connection, I figured, why not use it? And so I did, and because of that, the cash flowed in, and I could afford to buy myself pieces of happiness. Weed gave me the latest phone, nice clothes, and even another car. It allowed me to live a little more comfortable, attend the clubs more frequently, and enjoy things I never got to do before. And man, I'm not going to front, I had a ball.

The crazy part is that I was able to keep my weed hustle a secret. No one suspected what I was doing. Never did it cross anyone's mind that I was selling drugs. I was beginning to think that I was living the dream. But, I still needed more. Something bigger. I enjoyed rap and watching videos of my favorite artists such as Jay Z and Lil' Wayne. From those videos, and observing the lives of rappers, I realized that I wanted to mimic them. I wanted what they had. I wanted to be known. I wanted their status, money, and their lifestyle. To me, they had it all.

My dreams got bigger but were still grounded in some form of reality. Realistically, I knew that I was never going to reach millionaire status like the Diddy's or Jay Z's of the world. However, I did want to be "hood-rich". I wanted to be that guy that would turn heads when I would pull up in my car or show off my crib!

These were the goals I set for myself when I was 21. At this time in my life, I wanted the material things and all the flash. So, I partied hard and hustled even harder. I wanted to enjoy my best life. The world was mine, and I wanted a piece of it. I could somewhat afford to live the life that I dreamed of, so, I worked and hustled on the side. Most of my weekends were spent in Ybor City. This was the place that was known for their bars and clubs, and in my opinion, one of the best places to have a good time.

Every weekend, my boys from Orlando would come out with me and hit up the night scene there in Ybor City. Some nights we would roll 20 people deep. I always felt empowered when my homies came down. I felt like I couldn't be touched. I felt like I was somebody just because of the looks people would give me when we went out. We would drive down Ybor City's main strip with Maximas, Big Bodies, and Lexuses all decked with rims and TV's. In my mind, I was living the life. I sure felt hood-rich.

In order to create the persona that I was trying to build, I went and got myself some fronts. People around me were wearing gold teeth, so I figured I'd get me a pair. You can blame Paul Wall for the craze of fronts and gold teeth. My fronts were custom made gold fronts, white gold 6 on top, and I made sure that they were pineapple cut. With these fronts, I felt as if I was the hardest person out. Surprisingly, these fronts fit my style, and actually gave me the look and feel I aimed to create.

I had so many plans I wanted to accomplish, and though I

knew my lifestyle and choices were not the best, they were still too appealing and good for me to pass up and quit. One thing I wanted to do was to expand my connections and live even bigger. This is where dope came in. Quickly did I learn that weed could get clothes, but it was dope that got the houses and cars. So, selling weed led to selling dope.

In the past, I would have felt guilty for the types of choices and actions I was making, but the more I partied, the more my conscience was numbed. That small voice of reason was ignored, my conscience died down, and eventually it completely disappeared. Once that voice of reason quit guiding my thoughts, I ended up in a dangerous place–a place where my choices led towards destruction.

My life was slowly spiraling out of control, but I had no clue. I was living the boiling-frog myth, simmering gradually in my dysfunctions. The morals that I grew up with quit being my guide. Instead, I was functioning off of emotion and excitement, giving no regard to considering consequences of my choices.

Without hearing that small voice, I stopped choosing the best company. My choice crowd, who was the major influence for me at that moment of time, were people who didn't meet the morals and standards I had initially set for myself. And as a result, the influence that surrounded me was steering me away from becoming the type of person that deep down inside my heart I knew I needed to be. Without that small voice of reason, I began losing sight of why I originally moved to Tampa. Tampa was supposed to be a new start and a place for me to learn from my homeboy Wayne. Wayne actually saved money and didn't blow it, unlike me. Wayne made sure he finished school. He was focused, I was not. I was becoming the opposite of my Tampa dream and living for the moment. Listening to that small voice in my head was of utmost importance, and I flat out ignored and erased it.

On one particular day, I purchased a vehicle in Orlando. It was a big body car, just as I wanted. I had hopes of painting it black, adding some big boy rims, and turning it into my *dope boy* car. Everyone has to have their big boy car. This was going to be mine.

Immediately after purchasing this car, I excitedly took off in it. The car wasn't even registered or insured. But to me, those were minor details that didn't matter at the moment because I was under a time constraint. All I wanted to do was return to Tampa as quickly as possible so I could get it hooked up. There was one quick stop I needed to make on my trip back. I needed to refill my stash of supplies–weed and dope. My list of illegal activities were just stacking higher. Did I care? Nope. So, I made that quick stop anyway, and rushed my way home.

As my luck had it, within 15 miles of purchasing this vehicle, the motor blew! I was livid. Thankfully, I had AAA, so I hit them up, and waited by the side of the road for their tow truck to arrive. It was a hot day, as most Florida days are. So, I stepped out of my new broken car to catch a little breeze. After all, knowing the nature of towing companies, I knew there was a chance that I could be waiting for a long time. I sat on top of my trunk, fidgeting on my phone to make the minutes pass faster. Only a minute or two passed, and I noticed from far away that all-so-familiar black and white car with colored lights pull up behind me. *"D#$% last thing I need right now is the police asking any questions.* I had to play it smart, and I had to remain calm since I had a fake tag, no insurance, no registration, and the car I was sitting on was actually an old police car that had been auctioned off. "You okay sir?" the officer yelled as he stuck his head out of his window.

"Yup," I responded confidently. "My motor blew. Just waiting for the tow truck to haul me back to Tampa." There was a brief pause, and I waited in anticipation for the officer's response.

"Okay, good luck then." the officer wished me as he pulled away.

I breathed a sigh of relief. *That was close!* What just happened, NEVER happens, especially to Black people. All the officer had to do was ask for my license and registration, run the tag, or investigate my car, and I would have been done for. Then, this book would not exist. Some may call it luck; however, I call it providence. The fact that I didn't get caught, was evidence right there, that God had a plan for me despite all my foolish mistakes.

That day, I may have dodged the police, but my fast thrill-seeking life and recklessness did catch up with me eventually. One evening, shortly after the car-break-down moment, many of my Orlando boys were away celebrating a birthday in Daytona. For whatever reason, I was left behind. So, I decided to hit up the clubs with my co-workers instead. It was an ordinary evening. We pre-gammed, put on our outfits and headed off to party the night away at Ybor city.

One of my co-workers brought along a female friend that evening. Her name was Jessica.

She was super dope. Typical New York Puerto Rican girl who had swag, good looks, and someone I was definitely feeling. She was drop dead gorgeous. Jessica was in the music biz. She was friends with a well-known rapper from New York and even starred as a dancer in his music videos. It isn't every day you get to be out on a beautiful night with an attractive girl like her, so you know, yo boy had to shoot his shot. I did everything I could to make sure that she had a good time, from buying her drinks to cracking jokes. I wanted her to feel as comfortable as possible and have a dope of an evening.

What started as a fun night, quickly turned into a disaster. As soon as we walked into the club, we noticed a group of dudes with dreads hanging out by the entrance of the club. They noticed us too. More accurately, they noticed Jessica. These dudes approached Jessica. They acted friendly and tried to get her attention by hollering at her. Things escalated quickly, and what went from trying to get attention, morphed into all out harassment as the dreadheads began grabbing Jessica inappropriately. The more she continued to defend herself, the more the dreadheads got aggressive. Things were getting too hostile so, I stepped in to defend her. I positioned myself in between Jessica and the dreadheads, looked them in the eye with my gold fronts in my mouth, and mean-mugged them. I stood my ground, told them to be respectful, and warned them that if they weren't, they would have problems with me. Big talk for someone who didn't have his boys with him to back him up. However, defending friends is what I have done all my life. Being a one-man show wasn't going to change that.

Speaking of having big talk, I was actually so drunk at that hour. I don't remember if it was five minutes or five hours that passed from that big talk moment. Although, all I recall, was a tap on my shoulder, turning around, getting punched right in the face, and falling to the ground.

As I stood up, the group of dreadheads encircled me ready to fight. I quickly grabbed my roommate and his buddy and dragged them into my rising dilemma. My roommate had a beer bottle in his hand ready to go, and his buddy had a knife, which he managed to sneak into the club. Even with them there, we were still clearly outnumbered by around 15 to our 3. My heart was racing as I awaited the dreadheads' next move. Without delay, I mustered the courage to actually swing at one of them. As soon as this happened, the bouncer grabbed me and threw me out of the club.

Sitting outside of the club, I noticed that the parking lot was empty. I could hear the music blasting from the inside as I sat there by my lonesome. *Well, this sucks!* I snatched my phone from my back pocket and tried to call my boys in hopes that they would come help me out. *Ugh, they're in Daytona,* I remembered.

Shortly after, the news got to me that the dreadheads ended up beating Jessica to a bloody pulp. She had to be rushed to the hospital for the multiple fractions to jaw, nose, and ribs. As my heart broke hearing about what happened to Jessica, I couldn't help but imagine how much worse it would have been if I was there. God was looking out for me that night. If I hadn't gotten thrown out of the club, what would have happened to me? Would I also have had a fractured jaw and ribs? Or even worse, have died? Again, some may call this luck, but I called this providence.

Later that day, I awoke with one of the worst hangovers I have ever experienced in my life. My right eye was all shades of black, blue, and purple. I had never had anything like it. The reflection that I saw of me in the mirror looked like something out of a UFC fight. Both inside and out, I was crumbling into pieces. *Who was this person reflecting back at me from the mirror? Who was I becoming? What happened to that innocent Christian boy growing up with prayerful parents? Where did he go?*

The Good Book states that bad company corrupts good character. That's exactly what was happening to me. I had chosen bad company. As a result, my character was paying for it. Everything in my life at that moment was getting completely out of hand. If my younger self were to peek into the future and see my current self, that younger self would have been shocked, ashamed, and devastated. My choices led me here, turning me into someone I never thought I would develop into. My music and movies fueled this confused kid. Every decision I made really mattered. Decisions either helped mold me into a person of good standing that deep down inside I desired to be, or that dude that I never thought I would become. There is a principle that states that by beholding, you become changed. What I was beholding was violence, drugs, and cheap thrills. Thus, my life became one cheap thrill.

My life lacked focus and discipline. The opportunity for me to turn over a new leaf and create a life different was before me. However, I botched up that chance, didn't grind, and take advantage of my opportunities. I had a positive roommate, work opportunities, and a chance to receive an education, but I never used those tools to assist in building something beneficial for my future. Like the saying goes, "Old habits die hard." I was living proof of that.

There was a certain way I wanted people to perceive me, and I was too concerned about creating that image and having a good time. I wanted to look successful without having actual success. I was hustling but didn't know what I was hustling for. I wanted attention but was seeking it in all the wrong places. I was basically acting like a leaf tossed in the wind. One with no direction, substance or no real sense of purpose.

If I had just been a tad wiser, I would have used my same hustle mentality to finish school instead of selling drugs. If I had been a tad smarter, I would have utilized my same energy to pursue my hoop dreams rather than pouring it into partying and buying useless things. If I had just done all this, maybe I would have had perception that was real instead of fake.

Biggie Smalls once said, "The sky is the limit." The sky is where I believe I settled, not realizing that beyond the sky sits an entire universe. This vast universe was ready to be conquered, and I could have conquered it. But instead I only settled for what I could see at the moment–the sky.

It's unfortunate that my younger self was unable to go back in time and tell my old self to not make bad decisions. Unfortunately, there's no way to go back in the past, but what I can do, is take the lessons from the past, learn from them, and teach others not to make my same mistakes.

Don't do what I did. Don't be a confused Lo. Live out your life with purpose. By applying these simple points, I know that you can achieve your desired success.

- **Place yourself in a circle of friends who will push you to do better.** Surround yourself with people who daily strive to find ways to improve themselves and motivate you to do the same. (I had two sets of friends – grinders and partiers. The grinders were productive in creating enriching experiences with their lives. I chose to follow the partiers. When I did grind, it was so I could party.)

- **Develop principles that will govern your thoughts and actions.** Live firmly to these principles without compromise. (My family ingrained within me good moral principles, but I compromised them because I wanted glitter, flash, and exciting instant gain. Hence, why I chose to sell drugs.)

- **Seize every positive opportunity given to you.** If you have the chance to learn from a mentor, go to school, take a job, or anything that will help advance you in your goals, grab that opportunity. It may not come around again. Live for the future, not for the moment. (Learning from Wayne, making decent money, and attending school in Tampa was my chance for a fresh start, but I sacrificed it all because I was blinded by temporal happiness.) Keep in mind that there are no shortcuts in life. Jot down your priorities. As you are doing this, identify anything in your life that may need to be cut out because it could prevent you from achieving your big goal.

Your future is ahead of you. You are in control. You got this. Don't be like Lo-confused. Stay focused on the big picture and steer away from anyone or anything that will distract you from achieving the goals and greatness that you are capable of achieving. Remember, as you are planning the life you want ahead of you, reach beyond the sky and conquer the universe, and as you are doing this, always ask yourself this key question... Who am I?

QUESTIONS

- Have there been moments in your life where you ended up taking an unexpected path?
- If so, did you take steps to change the direction of your course? If you did, what were those steps?
- Describe the type of friends within your circle. Are they helping you reach your goals or distracting you?
- Are you satisfied with the person that you are today? Explain why or why not.
- What principles have you set out for yourself that will help you go in the path you want to go? What have you done to ensure that those principles won't be compromised?
- Create a list of both short and long-term goals. Look at your list, do your short-term goals align and support your long-term ones?

CHAPTER 6

DREAM CHASING

You are probably wondering why I included the previous chapter in my book. The answer is simple. I had a vision. Before moving to Tampa, my vision and desire was to play basketball professionally in Puerto Rico. This was my big dream.

I had always had this dream, but the months prior to pursuing it, I actually held a lucrative job at a Fortune 500 company. My first paycheck was money I never made before. I received $2,500 for only two weeks of work. What kind of person my age made this kind of money? Not a kid with no college education and real work experience, that's for sure. This job had a 401(k), retirement plan, and health insurance. Talk about benefits! I never had anything like this before in my life.

With the kind of money I was making, I didn't know what to do with myself. So, I purchased unnecessary things like 20' rims for my car, installed a TV on my dashboard, even hooked up a Playstation 2 (I'm really revealing my age at this point), and put it all in my whip. My money bought me things that most people my age wish they had. However, there was one problem. I wasn't happy. I may have possessed things that most people would want, but inside I was still empty. Why? Because I wasn't fulfilling my dream. The money was good, but I felt like I wasn't fulfilling my purpose in life. It's weird to say, but at that point in life, I would rather have been dead broke living my basketball dreams then working a good job making lots of money.

My job held me to strict hours. I had to work 10-12 hour shifts, meet deadlines, and other stressful tasks. I was never a 9:00–5:00 kind of guy. I dreaded sitting behind a computer monitor in an office waiting to clock out. I longed to be free, to make my own decisions, and take control of my life. I wanted to be my own boss, and not be bogged down by this boring inflexible job.

After 8 months of working at this Fortune 500 company, an opportunity for me to try out for the basketball league in Puerto Rico popped up. When that happened, I knew I had some huge decisions to weigh out. It was either my high-paying job or my basketball dream. I couldn't have both. With some thought, I made a choice, a very tough one. I quit the job that earned me a little over 40 grand a year (a lot for a 20-year-old with no college degree), and I went after what was in my heart. Surprisingly, many of my co-workers supported my decision. I think they were proud of me for pursuing a dream I had been chasing in my heart for so long. Deep down, they wouldn't have the courage to drop the job themselves and pursue their own dreams.

I'm aware that I could have easily taken time off of work to try out for the team, instead of flat out quitting my job. In fact, many people encouraged me to do so. But I knew that keeping my job would make it possible for me to have a fall back plan. I knew that I didn't want to have a fall back plan. If there was a job waiting for me back home, I knew that I wouldn't give the tryouts my all. I wanted to be all in, to put all my eggs in one basket, and pursue this one thing that I wanted to achieve. Now, most people would give you the opposite counsel from what I just did. Most people would hang on tightly to their fall back plan. However, from my perspective, 100 percent effort and focus cannot be channeled into something, when in the back of your mind, there comfortably sits that fall back plan. For me, having a fall back plan wouldn't work. Raising the stakes, and increasing the risk, actually propelled me to work harder. I was going to make a team and play in the Puerto Rican Basketball league.

To make my dream a reality, I trained hard over the summer,

working out at the local gym from 6 AM for morning runs and sweating it all the way until the evening. I had to put in work if I wanted to compete with the best. It was a good thing I had money saved up from my Fortune 500 job. It made it so that I didn't have to worry about finances during this time. Instead of working, I could pour my entire soul into training. My eye was on the prize, to make this team, and I remained focused and intentional with my exercise routines. This is the type of intense focus that is necessary for everyone to have when trying to reach their goals. I had it.

At the end of the summer, off I went to Puerto Rico where tryouts were going to be held at a coliseum in Ponce. Embarking on this new dream and adventure was exciting, yet, I was still quite nervous and anxious. Over 500 athletes were invited to the tryouts, but only 50 would be drafted. If I wanted to be part of that 50, I knew I had to bring my A-game.

Day one of tryouts began. The gym was packed with top athletes from all over the country. I walked on to the newly polished gym floor, picked up a basketball, and tried to ease my nerves by shooting a few free throws. I scanned the crowd of my competitors. They all seemed to carry a chip on their shoulder. Most of the players were better, faster, stronger, and even more conditioned than me.

Despite all that, I still felt confident. As long as I had the right opportunity, I knew I could at least showcase my talent.

There may have been 500 of us there, but I knew I had a good shot at being one of those 50. Thanks to an event that transpired a week prior, I had a healthy confidence in myself knowing that I could compete with top talent. Back home in Orlando, I often played at a church where they would have open runs. To my surprise, two weeks before I headed off to Puerto Rico, a Puerto Rico legend and NBA star came and joined us on the court.

Puerto Rico tryouts were around the corner, so, I was eager to play against this legend and see how I matched up with his level of play. Defense wasn't my specialty. However, all the boys on the court knew I was heading to Puerto Rico for tryouts, so, they let me do my thing on offense instead. I was stoked. How often does one get to ball with a b-ball star?

It was a fast-paced game. The NBA player was swift, but I kept up. If there was any form of athleticism that he may have lacked, he sure compensated for it with experience. He had a quick first step and utilized his strength to maneuver himself to the spots he wanted to get to. On the flip side, I lacked both experience and technique, but I did make up for it with my awesome jump shot. My jumper was something that I worked on. To perfect my form, I mimicked shooters like Houston and Billups. That day, I brought on my best offense game. The basket was an ocean, and the ball was a pebble. As the game continued, I knew I had struck Arroyo's attention because he ended up guarding me. When the best player wants to guard you, then you know you have earned their attention and respect. The Puerto Rican legend and I were the show of that game, and everyone knew why.

That evening, we played a series of games. They were all close and competitive. Unfortunately, we lost all the games by one point each. To me, the scores didn't matter, because at the end of the runs, I earned the respect of the NBA legend. For me, this was the ultimate win.

The confidence boost of that experience with the player kept me level-headed as I went out to compete for one of those coveted 50 spots. I knew I possessed the talent, but could I get the scouts' attention? Some insight into these open tryouts, many of these scouts already have specific athletes they are watching. Often, they actually know ahead of time who they want to draft. So, don't think for one moment it's a fair playing field. It ain't!

Early on during tryouts, I ran the drills and got winded. They ran a lot of plays that day. Throughout them all, my nerves kept getting the best of me, counteracting my confidence, and screwing with my game. I kept on over thinking and missing my shots. What typically came easy for me seemed to be difficult to do. I was all thrown off. I struggled to keep up with the plays and drills they were calling out. My conditioning also wasn't as great as I anticipated, so I was too busy trying to catch my breath and couldn't fully grasp what they were saying. It was bad.

When the drills ended, it was time for open runs. During these open runs, you get to choose who to guard. As this was happening, I noticed there was one particular player everyone seemed to avoid. It was this guy who played for a D-1 school up north. Rumor had it that there was already a prospective team looking to sign him on. Made sense. Who wants to purposely put himself in a position to be embarrassed? On any other given day, I would have joined the crowd and avoided him too. But today was not any ordinary day for me. This was the day I had to bring on my best *A game* and get noticed. An idea struck. This dude, that everyone avoided, was my key. The opportunity to put me on the scouts' spotlight. As mentioned earlier, I wasn't the strongest defender, but I knew if I defended this guy, made his job a little harder on the court, and caused him to work for his shots, then scouts would notice me. For sure.

With this seemingly flawless new strategy in hand, I regained my confidence, and walked straight up to this dude. We introduced ourselves. His name was Alex, and we chatted for bit. Alex also happened to be one of the few English speaking players present at this tryout.

Before we began our runs, Alex asked me with a puzzled look on his face, "No disrespect, but why are you guarding me?" I replied, "I guess the others are just afraid of the spotlight. You might get the best of me, but just know you are going to work for everything you get!" I played the hardest defense I ever played in my life. I knew that in order to get noticed, or receive any shine or recognition, my best chance was on the defense end of the court. Alex played a tough game, but I made him work for every bead of sweat. My plan somewhat worked, for several of the scouts who were looking to sign Alex on, were impressed with the defense I played on him.

Tryouts ended, and the cuts were being made. The time came for those 50 names to be posted. I stood in front of the board of names and scanned my eyes down the list, hoping to see my name. *Did I make the cut? Did the scouts notice me? Had all my efforts paid off?*

I reached the bottom of the list of 50 names. No Lo-Ammi Richardson on the list. My heart sank. My dreams were crushed. With my head hung low, I turned and began to walk away. Just then, a voice echoed through the gym yelling, "Lo, you made it!" It was one of the guys I was bunking with. *What? How could that be?* I quickly ran back to the board, placed my finger on the first name, and ran it down rescanning through the list of names again, except this time, more carefully. There it was! Sure enough! My name! *How could I have missed it the first time?* It was there! Sure enough, I made the top 50. I was coming back for day 2.

Unless one has been in my same shoes, one will never understand the rush of emotions I experienced at that moment when I discovered that I qualified for the top 50 out of 500. Making it to the top 50 doesn't guarantee being signed on to a team. It just gives one a much better shot at making it to a team, a promotion to day 2 of tryouts, and an invitation to the big draft night. This was the process to get drafted on to a team. I had just made it past the first major step.

Day 2 of tryouts were just as intense as day 1. On this day, scrimmages and drills take place on the court similar to the day before. Except this time, competition is against the best of the best. We scrimmaged all day in a tournament style play. All 50 players were broken down into different teams and we competed. After the games were done, MVP awards were given to players within each bracket.

Day 2 of tryouts are also when scouts look for *hidden*

gems. If one is lucky, one may even get a personal invite to a team practice. These personal invites to team practices were important because it meant that a specific team had you pegged as a *gem player.* These open practices were the key to getting signed on to the team extending the invitation.

After tryouts, I was invited to a few team practices from teams that were interested in me, but I didn't accept any of the invitations. Sounds crazy to have turned down these invitations, right?! However, regardless of the fact that I had made it this far, I still didn't feel like any team had a genuine interest actually drafting me. So, *why warrant my time? These teams wouldn't take a shot at me anyway!* These were the thoughts of doubt milling through my head. Many people would think I was crazy to have shot down these offers. Perhaps I should have taken them up just to and see what would have panned out. However, in my mind, the experience of tryouts in itself was satisfying enough. Oddly enough, I was content with where I was, content with the tryout experience, and not moving forward.

Following day 2 of tryouts for the top 50 was this invitation to draft night. I received my invitation. This was the big evening. The big evening that would change the lives of many athletes forever. Here at draft night, players would wait to hear their names called by the team that selected them. Then, the official signing on to a team would take place. This ended the drafting process and marked the beginning of a new basketball career for many.

So, why didn't I get signed? For starters, I didn't attend open practices or even draft night. I didn't get the vibe that I actually had a real shot of getting drafted. Sadly, my gut was telling me that attending this camp was a useless effort. Why? Because my chances of getting drafted weren't 100%. Why waste my time doing something I felt wasn't solid?

I was so close. I had made it this far. Professional basketball was within my reach. The opportunity was sitting at my fingertips. One could almost smell that jersey with my number etched on it. This was the moment to work harder and make it on to a team. But I didn't. I could have seized that opportunity. But I didn't. Instead, having the satisfaction that I could make it was good enough for me. I know this wasn't the mindset I should have possessed, but I didn't really feel like I was going to get a fair shot. The last thing I wanted to do was be one of those players chasing a dream that wouldn't ever happen.

My issue, as mentioned in the previous chapter, was that I was looking for what basketball could bring me instead of the lesson I could learn from playing the game. I wanted the fame, money, but not the work that came with playing the game of basketball.

What do I mean? Basketball legends like MJ, Kobe (RIP to the Black Mamba) and Lebron take their passion of basketball and make it their lifework. These legends are constantly studying, perfecting their craft, and outworking their opponents. They never cheated themselves from the grind because they wanted to be considered one of the best of all time. For each of them, their hard work paid off. They polished their skills, and became world-renowned names, and as a result got the other perks like the cars, endorsements, houses, and the fame.

For me, I was willing to work hard, but not hard enough. It was all about doing enough just to get by. I wasn't in love with the game, but instead, wanted what the game could give me. My intrinsic motivation was lacking, and rather was focused on the extrinsic rewards.

Working out was a chore, and I did it only because I had to. I never pushed myself to the limit. I never maximized my full potential. Many people saw great potential in me, but I didn't see it in myself.

I made short cuts because my goals were short term. One has to fall in love with the process in order to be able to appreciate the glory. I didn't.

Looking back, I was scared. I was afraid of the possibilities of the unknown, of opening up my life to something foreign and different. What if I fell in love with the grind? What if I fell in love with sacrificing? What if I took the effort to focus on the small details? Could I have achieved more? Could I have done something greater? I believe I could achieved more and done greater things, but unfortunately I will never know. Certain windows of opportunities have passed, and I made my choices.

I cut myself short of greatness because I allowed glory to drive me, not my passion, and not my calling. Don't do the same. Achieve your greatness, seize those opportunities, and reach for those stars. This is how you find your purpose and identity. Then, you will be ultimately fulfilling what you were created to be.

As I reflect and think of what could have been, I remember having the right mindset, goals and dreams, but not the right work ethic. I loved the idea of achieving my dream and was willing to give up everything for it. However, when it came down to discipline and sacrifice, I didn't fall in love with that. Many people don't achieve their goals because they aren't willing to sacrifice everything necessary to achieve them. There were flashes where I could see my dreams being fulfilled, where I could smell it and what could be. But I never went the extra mile to make that flash be a constant light. Because of all this, I fell short of my dream.

So, how do dreams become reality, and how is greatness attained? Here are some tips that I have learned while reflecting upon my journey:

- **Find your dreams. Invest in them.** There are no shortcuts to dreams. Be willing to give up everything to pursue those dreams. Fall in love with the grind, the everyday struggles, the sacrifices, and ultimately the path that leads you to the greatness you desire. During those moments when you want to give up, find a way to fall in love with those moments. It's during our darkest times that we appreciate the light at the end of the tunnel. Remember there's always sunshine after the rain. Know what doesn't kill will you only make you stronger. Just as a seed needs to be buried in order for it to grow, bear in mind, that glory is often found amongst trying moments. So, push yourself through those difficult times.

- **Don't settle for anything less than what you want to achieve**. Make use of every opportunity given to you. Set high standards and hold yourself to them.
- **Be a learner!** Learn from other people's successes, achievements and failures. In order to be the best you can be, you must learn from the best. Find those people. Be around them. Immerse yourself in growing and perfecting the craft that you have been gifted with. Read, watch videos, ask questions and create a network of people who you can share your thoughts, ideas and struggles with. When I trained, I sought advice and tips from people who played professionally. I trained with these professionals, watched them play, and asked them questions I felt was necessary for me to expand my knowledge of the game. Never settle or become complacent with your efforts. Keep on learning. By doing this, you will be pushing forward towards the greatness you want to achieve. Never get to the point where you feel you have arrived or that you have made it. Learning is a process and not a destination.
- **Create a list of goals. Then, write a list of short term sacrifices you are willing to make in order to accomplish that goal.** Often times, people yearn for the glory but dodge the tedious tasks necessary to get there. Don't be that person. Tackle those tedious tasks. Make those sacrifices even if it means forgoing the snooze button, skipping the fast food, and turning

down the chance to hang out with friends. Keep those goals at the forefront of your mind. Recognize that sacrificing short term happiness may be what it takes to meet your goals and have long term success.

- **Character counts.** Character and mindset will determine your work ethic. Character is formed by hard, stern battles with self and overcoming your self-doubts. One must criticize themselves closely and not allow bad traits to remain uncorrected. Meditation is key to developing the character needed. In order to become a better version of yourself, take time to reflect on short comings and seeking ways to overcome those poor traits. There must be an earnest purpose to carry out the master plan that you have set up for yourself. Put in earnest, careful, persevering effort to break away from bad habits and associations that will sway you away from your goal. Form that character that counts. So, consider the type of character you need to develop in order to achieve your goals. As mentioned in this chapter, I started off with the right attitude, but not the right work ethic. Learn from me and go the extra mile. Take that extra step. Achieve that goal by being willing to go the extra mile. Too often we are satisfied with what could have been instead of what was achieved. That mindset is the difference between success and failure. One of my favorite phrases teaches that actions repeated form habits, habits form character, and by the character our destiny is decided.

Now, if only I had followed the same advice back then that I'm now giving. If I had done this, I wonder how life would have been different. I can't change the past, but I do wish I could go back and do things over, for I'm curious to what could have been. I want to go back to dream chasing!

QUESTIONS

- What goals have you set up for yourself?
- Have you accomplished your goals? If so, describe your feelings the moment you accomplished your goals.
- Have you ever been in a situation where you chose the shortcut over the difficult road?
- Share what this experience was like. How do you think things would have turned out if you took the difficult road instead?
- In your opinion, what should I have done differently?

CHAPTER 7

I'M BACK!

It was March 18, 1995 when the world heard the two most famous words uttered by the NBA's greatest player, Michael Jordan, "I'm back." This was Michael Jordan's historic announcement as he returned to play for the Chicago Bulls after only being in retirement for nearly three years.

Those two words, "I'm back" deeply resonated with me because they perfectly described my return back home to Orlando after living in Tampa for over a year. Like Jordan facing a new start, I experienced feelings of excitement and anticipation during my drive from home from Tampa to Orlando.

Though Tampa definitely had its pros, there was nothing like returning to the city I loved. Orlando was home. Orlando was the city that shaped me and filled my life with the most memories. Moving back to Orlando was a no brainer.

Tampa never felt like home to me. Even though Tampa came with the thrill of moving to a new city and having the chance of a new start, it still wasn't enough. It just wasn't home.

While in Tampa, I could see myself heading down the wrong path. Moving back home to Orlando was the fix. I knew I had to reroute myself in order to prevent from straying even more into the wrong direction. I had to switch my focus, and I knew that moving back to Orlando would help me do that. Hence, back to Orlando I went.

One of my favorite activities during my 20's was going to clubs. It was a package deal of all of thrills: women, liquor, chillin' with celebs and hangin' out with the homies. However, after awhile, even the club scene lost its appeal and got boring. There's only so many VIP's one can go to, and celebrities to meet, before one seeks and desires something new. That's where I found myself during the summer of '09, in search for a new scene.

The scenery for me changed that summer, (which was probably one of the best summers of my life) when I was introduced to the college bar scene. The college bar scene was super dope with its smaller crowds, new people, beautiful college women, and amazing drink specials. One of my good friends was a popular DJ, and every time he worked, I got in the bars and drank for free. The environment was friendlier than the clubs I frequently attended in the past. It was also nice not having my track record, for altercations followed me to these bars. That was a plus. The college bar scene brought me some of the best times of my life.

During this time in my life, the problem I was facing was that I had developed an alcohol dependency, but I was completely oblivious to that fact. Drinking was infused into pretty much every part of my life. From work, outings, and even basketball games, alcohol was always a part of it all. I typically would pre-game before going out for the night. Then, the drinks would continue once my buddies and I hit the bar. My habit of drinking continued to grow. I would drink when I went out to eat. After work, I would drink for happy hour. At the beach, I would drink and have a 12-pack of beer in deck. Ball games, particularly, was where I would get the most lit. Every occasion warranted a drink in hand. No matter what I was doing, the bottom line was, I drank. Period!

Alcohol always put me in a chill mood. It allowed me to escape whatever issues I was facing at the moment. I didn't always know what I was escaping, but whatever it was, alcohol was my go to. Having alcohol in my system automatically put me in a better mood. All of my *fun* memories came at the expense of alcohol. It didn't matter what I was doing, or even drinking. A drink just equaled a good time for me.

Eventually, my drinking habit took its toll on me, and caused me to have a different outlook on life. One night, some of my boys and I decided to check out a new club in town. Before doing this, Will, a good friend of ours, stopped by my crib to have a drink and show off the new gun he had just purchased. We were standing outside of the apartment complex, drinks in hand, admiring this new purchase of his. Will shot off a few warning shots so we could see the gun in action. Stereotypically, young African-Americans, who own guns are often portrayed as thugs or criminals. That wasn't us. None of us there were killers or gangsters, but all of us had the smarts to know that in order to be safe we had to stay protected and strapped. Protection, that's what Will's gun purchase was all about. I know my boy. He didn't purchase the gun for any other reason except for protection.

After Will showed off his new gun purchase, we hopped into our cars and drove off to check out the new club in town. I specifically had a conversation with my boys telling them to chill out and not get ourselves into any trouble. We couldn't afford it. This was a new club, new crowd, and we didn't know the people that were there. Everyone agreed to stay low key for the night and just enjoy the festivities. I don't know what possessed me to have that conversation, but later on, I realized that it was providence.

We arrived at the new club. It was a new spot on I-Drive near all the tourist spots in Orlando. It was a fun night; everyone was enjoying themselves. The music, company and special drinks made the night memorable. As the night progressed, I saw my boy, Lac, talking to this cute girl from his neighborhood. All was cool until this girl's man showed up. Mind you, Lac knew this girl, and this girl knew him. From a distance, it just looked like they were catching up, joking, and laughing. There wasn't any funny business going on between them. They were just having a good time. I watched at a distance as the boyfriend approached the two who were having a conversation. The boyfriend walked confidently towards them, stood behind his girl, and casually put his hand around her shoulder. Just like that, this cute chic did a 180, and acted like Lac had been harassing her the whole night as if he knew she had a boyfriend.

This girl was lying straight up! I saw her with my very own eyes. She went out of her way to holler at my boy! This was all on her! She could have easily told the truth. Maybe the boyfriend was the jealous type? I don't know, but the situation escalated, and things got heated quickly. It was like a scene from a bad reality show on VH-1 that turned dramatic and hostile. It went from trying to resolve the situation to finger pointing. Then, it quickly escalated to yelling, cursing and threats between Lac and the boyfriend. The situation got to the point where the bouncers had to escort Lac and the boyfriend out of the club. When this happened, I rounded up the rest of the crew. We chugged our drinks and headed outside the club to try to resolve the situation at hand.

We didn't have a big group with us. Usually, there are more of us hanging out, but tonight we were a group of 5. As we were exiting the club, we noticed a lot of commotion. In order to try to maneuver around people, we had to shove and bump them out the way, which caused people to spill their drinks. We did all this just to make it to the spot where the confrontation was taking place. Once we got there, we jumped in and tried our best to calm the situation down. However, our efforts failed, and things got progressively worse. The boyfriend and Lac were still exchanging words. Things got even more heated. There was a lot of yelling and even more cursing. Then came the threats. We tried having them handle the situation themselves. But that didn't work. Lac took off his shirt and threw a wild punch in the boyfriend's direction. Before we knew it, a full-on fight broke out.

The crazy part was seeing Lac's brother ball up his fist waiting in anticipation for the boyfriend to come in his direction while calculating the perfect time to throw a punch. He did and perfectly landed a solid blow right on the boyfriend's nose causing his nose to break. Instantly blood was scattered everywhere. After that occurred a full-on WWE Wrestle Mania-type of fight broke out.

Punches were coming from every direction. Things got so bad it felt like we were fighting a defeated battle. I didn't care to get involved in the fight, but I had to in order to pull Lac away from all the chaos. Then, the thought struck me. *The gun, it's in the trunk of the car!*

Will had placed the gun in the truck. The gun was tucked away where nobody could get access to it easily. *I figured it was the solution to resolve this situation.* Out of an impulse of anger, I asked Lac, who had blood all over him, "Dude, where's the keys?" Lac looked at me dazed and confused. So, I asked the question again. He kept patting his pockets indicating that the keys were there. I reached for the keys from his pocket, but they weren't there. "Lac, the keys ain't there!"

"D$&* it, they must have fallen out man!" Lac answered back. All I could do was curse at that moment. I ran away from the fight scene and headed to the car anyways. On my way there, I kept looking at the ground searching for the keys. *Maybe they fell out of his pocket.* I was desperate to find those keys. Then just like that, I spotted the keys laying on the parking lot floor. I picked them up and quickly opened the trunk, where the gun was hidden. All I wanted was to get the gun in my hand. Now, I didn't have a plan on what exactly to do with the gun once I found it. But I knew I needed it. I reached my hand into the spot where Lac placed the gun, and to my surprise, it was gone! *What the &$#@ ! It was just here! Where'd it go?* I ran back to the fight scene. I was so irritated that I couldn't find the gun, and the plan didn't go as I would have liked.

To this day, I don't know where the gun went and how it mysteriously disappeared. Perhaps my memory was off, maybe it got stolen, but the disappearance still remains a mystery. The missing gun was a blessing though because who knows what would have happened if that gun had made it into my raging hands. Some call it luck, but I call what happened, providence.

This wasn't the first time I went through a situation like this, one where the Man upstairs seemingly intervened and saved me from greater trouble. One would also think that I'd learn from the mistakes of my previous experiences, but that's not the case with me. For example, earlier that year after, I found myself in the middle of a similar situation back in Orlando as I was leaving Club Paris (another club different from the one mentioned above). I got into a confrontation that led to bats being pulled out and gun shots being fired at the car as we were driving.

When MJ made the decision to return to Chicago after his retirement, he was still MJ. He was still the goat. He was still the big shot maker fans were accustomed to seeing. However, when he returned, he had a different number. He was #45, and not #23! He may have had the same name, but the number didn't fit him. Everyone was accustomed to the legendary #23. The fans were looking for #23. But he was #45. It just wasn't the same. This was my same experience. I knew Orlando, but actions weren't what people were accustomed to seeing me doing. Just as MJ changed, wearing #45 back to #23, I reverted to the old me, the Orlando me because the Tampa me just didn't fit right. Yes, in some ways I had changed, but not for the better. I was still basically the same old me, back in Orlando, back to what was familiar. I was still lost. I still had no identity. I did not know who I was, and I sure wasn't living to what Lo-Ammi was created to be.

I had enjoyed the innocence of life. I was known as the life of the party. I was known as someone who knew everyone, and everyone knew me. I had connections with people, but at the end of the day, I was waking up with no purpose. Being dependent on thrills, women, alcohol and other short-lived excitements caused me not to be able to live my best life. Reflecting back, I realize that the moments in which I had God and family were the times when I was fully living out my purpose and understanding my identity. Family, friends and purpose are so important in order for one to live the life they are intended to live.

Know your purpose. Without purpose, one will find themselves doing everything within their power to live for the thrill. Life is much more than thrills. Thrills leave emptiness, and purpose gives you drive.

The summer of '09 was one of my most thrilling summers. It held the best memories of my life. That summer was the epitome of clubs, bars, jokes, laughs, and countless memories with friends. When I stop to reminisce of that summer, I think to myself, "Man, I did have fun." However, what people didn't see beneath the surface was the hurt I experienced when I had some friendships that ended, witnessed marriages that failed, watched friends dealing with depression, seeing homeboys die, and having close female friends get knocked up and have to raise that child on their own. The instant thrills caused a life full of sorrow and agony for me. This hurt and brokenness I experienced led me to be dependent on alcohol and various other thrills of life.

Many young people in their teens and young adult life fall into the same trap that I did–the thrill trap. Within this thrill trap comes an addiction to something in hope to escape an undesired reality. This thrill trap also brings on a lack of purpose.

Deep down, during this supposedly *best summer of my life*, I still longed for acceptance. Deep down, I desired to be loved. I needed this in my life, so I did what I needed to do in order for me to experience both love and acceptance. I sought it in sex, alcohol, parties, and more. However, none of these thrills filled the void that I so desperately needed to be filled. Through this experience, I discovered that bad habits just ended up creating more problematic situations in the future.

Changing my location, did not help me escape my past. The solution was not that simple, and required deep soul searching. The problem rested within the habits that fabricated my core being.

My choices led me down a path of unhappiness and lack of fulfillment. The memories of that time were still precious. I loved my friends and the memories of the past I shared with them. But peeling off all the thrilling layers, the truth of that summer's experience was that I was still looking for myself, searching for happiness, seeking identity, and trying to discover a purpose.

Michael Jordan retired from the game of basketball because he was trying to escape the reality of dealing with his own drama–his father's death. Everyone knew MJ never really fit in or looked right in a baseball uniform. That's not what he was created to be. He was created to be a basketball player. He tried changing his number, but he quickly realized that if he was going to be the greatest to ever play the game, he would have to go back to what he knew, and what he was familiar with. So #45 worked for a moment, but wearing #23 reminded him of who he really was and what he was remembered for. Ponder upon these questions:

- What gets you up in the morning?
- What's your source of motivation?
- What currently drives you to make your daily choices and decisions?

It's so easy to follow the flow, be blown by the wind of circumstances and immediate thrills, that core questions such as the ones above are never pondered. Because often, time is not taken to reflect and answer these questions. This is why there is no understanding of purpose.

Remember, you can change your circumstances, but in order to do this, the changes must begin within you. Change your thinking. Change your outlook. Don't rely on your circumstances to make that change. What are you created to be? Are people determining your choices or behavior patterns? Look beyond the thrills, what are you wanting to do to change the world?

Bad habits stem from a void of something lacking in your experience. It may be the absence of love, confirmation, security, identity, purpose, or something else. Break those bad habits, whatever they are, by going on a limb and engaging in something you wouldn't normally do. Trade in that bottle of beer for a game night with family or friends. Choose a concert or attend a festival instead of a club. Do the opposite of what you would normally do. Choose wholesomeness instead of brokenness.

Simplify your life. Plan things that would encourage positive behavior that won't cause you to be dependent on other substances such as alcohol, drugs, and porn. Make moves that focus on bettering the inner person. Happiness isn't necessarily brought by memories, fun times or stimulating events. Happiness can also be brought by staying true to who you are and being what you were created to be.

Don't waste your life on the opinions of others, or what culture defines you should be. You were created to love and be loved. Don't escape the responsibility of bettering yourself because you feel like you may fail. Failure only comes because you don't try.

Be great! Strive for greatness and go back to the basics of what brings true happiness. And, before you know it, you'll be saying the same phrase as MJ, "I'm back!"

QUESTIONS

- What part of the story do you relate with?
- Have you ever been driven by the entertainment of life instead of the purpose you were created to be?
- What are some keys to making life simple and fulfilling without having to compromise the person you were created to be?
- Why do you think drugs, sex and alcohol are always advertised as the things needed for life fulfillment?
- Why do you think we as a society gravitate to the things that are labeled as bad, but glorified as good, instead of enjoying the simplicity of life?
- Have you been desensitized to what culture equates to happiness?

CHAPTER 8

WHAT IS THE MEANING OF LIFE? 808 AND HEARTBREAKS

She was one of the prettiest girls I ever laid my eyes on – long black hair, and the cutest dimples ever. She had a gorgeous captivating smile and a magnetic personality. Her name was Eden. Eden had just moved from New York to Orlando and attended my boot camp class where I was currently working as a personal trainer. I figured that if I couldn't make it as a professional athlete, the next best thing would be to train those in the making. My heart was in athletics, and I loved being surrounded in the athletic world. So, for the time being, personal training was a perfect fit.

Eden was different from all the other girls I had ever met. She didn't party, didn't curse, and attended church regularly. She was the very opposite of me and my life. It was crazy to see someone actually living the kind of life I should have been practicing.

Since my move from Tampa, I had spent many moments reflecting upon my time there, gathering lessons, and formulating a self-improvement list. Idle time was my enemy, so to be productive, I wrote this list. Upon completion, my list basically had one item. Item #1 on the agenda stated the following: Get into less trouble.

My strategy to achieve this important self-improvement goal was to avoid the clubs and go to bars instead. The bar scene was a much better environment and choice for me. Going to the bars helped me to achieve the goal of being low-key and staying out of trouble. I never thought about being in a committed relationship.

My interactions with Eden were limited, sparse, and contained within the four walls of the gym room. I remained cordial with her as I was with all my other students who had signed up for my boot camp class. However, as time progressed, our interactions continued, and I got to know her a little bit better. My interest in her grew.

I made up my mind to ask Eden out on a *date*– the kind of *date* that's really not a date, but kinda is. So, I finally mustered up the courage to ask if she was interested in seeing the best that Orlando had to offer. To my surprise, she said, "Yes." So, I took her on the-unofficial-show-her-around-town kind of date.

It was a Thursday afternoon and I had just finished my last boot camp session. My heart raced as I drove over to pick Eden up from her aunt's house. Our date began with me showing her around town to some of Orlando's coolest sites. We went to Universal City Walk for dinner, watched a movie, and just enjoyed our time together. Our conversations were flowing, and the night couldn't have been any better. Every time she smiled, her dimples made my heart skip a beat. She was nothing short of stunning and being with her made time stand still.

This one date led to a few others, which then led to countless hours talking on the phone. Our conversations would last till 3am and end with the "You hang up"... "No, you hang up….." "No, you hang up first." The typical teenage bopper type romance.

I had fallen in love. Yes, Lo-ammi, in love. The whole butterflies in my stomach, can't stop thinking of her missing her once I got off the phone type of love. She made up for all the bad things that were happening in my life.

When I had met Eden, I was in a tough spot in my life. It seemed as though whenever something good was happening, it would be counteracted by a series of random frustrating events that took a mental and emotional toll on me. Bizarre things would occur such as my car would break down or money that I had saved disappeared because of random bills that would unexpectedly show up in my mail. It seemed as though eviction notices were frequently posted on my door and my electricity and gas kept being cut off. At that time, I had five people living with me, all of whom, were struggling financially, dumping many burdens on me. It was as if I was taking on the responsibility of supporting all 5 people.

My life felt like it was falling into pieces, but thankfully Eden was around. I was far from put together, and she was all put together in nice packaging complete with a ribbon on top. She completed me. She was everything I wasn't. Eden brought light to my darkness. She made things make sense when nothing else did.

Eden popped into my life when I needed her most. She didn't know this, but she was my saving grace at that moment in time. Not only was my living situation a mess, but emotionally, my perception and perspective around me had become different. No matter how many bars I hopped, I just wasn't having fun like I had been in the past. Partying just wasn't what it used to be. All that I considered fun, such as drinking, clubbing and sex still brought me emptiness. Not everything that glittered felt like gold. Emptiness always followed. I felt empty. Something was definitely missing, but I couldn't put my finger on what it was. Having Eden in my life changed everything, for when I was with her, all that emptiness disappeared. With her in my life, I felt rejuvenated, as if I had something to live for again.

Eden became my world. My entire life revolved around her. She was the reason I woke up each morning. It was the image of her smiling face that would give me a needed boost of motivation. She was like the caffeine to my coffee, the person that kept me warm when Mondays and Tuesdays grew cold. All the wrongs in my life, she seemed to make right. Eden was my everything and became my purpose and my reason for life's existence.

My life may not have been the greatest, but this relationship was like icing that masked all the ugliness. So, I channeled all my energy, trust, and money in maintaining this relationship. As long as I was with her, nothing else mattered.

Then it happened, just when things appeared to be going great. In my mind, I was already planning on marrying Eden. But then, it happened, and changed my life forever.

One weekend, Eden traveled uptown for a few days with one of her friends. Before leaving, she had warned me that where she was going, the reception was going to be poor. So, when I didn't hear from her all weekend, it didn't surprise me. But then, Monday came and passed, and I still hadn't heard from her. *Odd*. Tuesday swung by, and still nothing. Not a word. Finally, on Wednesday, I received a vague text message informing me that her phone was out of service and that she would connect with me later.

Aha! Phew, I knew it. No signal, I thought to myself, offering myself some sort of comfort or consolation for the excruciating and mysterious dead silence I just lived through.

But then, it happened. An email popped into my inbox – one that shattered my world. The email went something like this:

To: Loammi@mail.me
From: butterflylove1587@hotmail.com

Dear Lo,
Something happened over the weekend that really opened my eyes. For the majority of my 20s, I've been in a relationship, and it seems like you are ready to settle down. I'm not ready for that again. Sorry, but I realized that I'm not ready for a relationship. I think we should kind of back off a bit. I feel it's better we not communicate and just be friends.

Sincerely,
Eden

What!!! What happened? What went wrong?! That email was like a dagger to my heart. Questions and doubts crept in.

How could she feel this way? Especially after all the intimate moments we shared? How is this possible? How could she feel any differently about me then what I felt about her?

I responded to her email, asking her all the questions that plagued my mind. I waited anxiously for a response, sitting there hitting the refresh button on my inbox page hoping that another email would show up. Silence. I never got an answer. She left me hanging and hurt with absolutely no closure. I never discovered why she ended things with me. All I know is that she moved back to New York. Years later, I did learn that she married her ex, the same guy that she originally moved from New York to escape.

Depression hit, and it hit me hard. I felt like sleeping and hoping I would never wake up again. Life had lost its meaning. The one thing that was my saving grace now felt like a death sentence looming over my head. My blessing felt like a curse. It was a heartbreak I didn't think I could ever recover from.

Instead of dealing with the pain, emptiness, and heartache, I found my escape through binge watching "The Office" and getting lost in the show. The chemistry between Jim and Pam's innocent flirtations. Dwight Schrute's endless bag of antics and oddities and the dead-pan humor of the entire staff became my diversion from reality and the temporary healing balm to my broken heart.

Many young people may be able to relate with my reasons and form of escape. Often Netflix and other media outlets serve as virtual spaces of refuge that aid in diminishing the hurts of reality. People find comfort in listening to music that relates to their pain that they experienced. Romantic movies are watched to give hope that Prince Charming does exist. People turn to porn because of the addictive satisfaction and pleasure it brings. Drugs numb pain and video games allow one to enter into another better world. All these cures may mask pain, but I found that it never fixes it.

Loneliness and emptiness are dangerous. I know this first-hand. If not addressed and dealt with properly, it can often lead to depression, and in some worse cases, even suicide. If you ever find yourself experiencing any form of depression, find someone you trust, and talk to them. It may be a professional, or even a friend. Just don't hold it in. Don't ever let things come to the point where you feel there is no escape. There are people and tools available to help you. Time also is a curer of pain and a key to survival. I wish someone had told me all this. I wish someone had been there to listen to me and allow me to open up and reveal my pain. I wish someone was present back then to understand what I was going through. That would have been a better healing balm and a much more effective means of escape. Not "The Office."

Once "The Office" ended, I was dumped back into the aching realities of life, and found myself asking the following questions: What is the meaning of life? Why am I even here? Why does everything good end up bad for me? Why can't I seem to catch a break?

Then, I received a call from my sister that would radically change my life forever!

QUESTIONS

- What do you think is the meaning of life?
- Have you experienced emptiness, heartache, pain, depression or even suicidal thoughts? If so, why do you think you are experiencing these emotions? What have you done to overcome those emotions and thoughts?
- Have you found yourself placing your trust, love, and care in the hands of an individual? If so, how many times have you found yourself in that situation? What was that like?

CHAPTER 9

DEAD AND GONE

In 2009, rapper T.I. released the single "Dead and Gone" featuring Justin Timberlake. In the song, he addresses the death of his best friend and former bodyguard, Philant Johnson, who was killed on May 3, 2006. Producer Rob Knox expressed his thoughts on why the song was created. He stated, "This guy's [T.I] was going through a lot with his whole court case situation and his best friend dyin', and everything in the world kind of crumbling in front of him in a way. We [agreed] it would be cool and unexpected to give people something a little more heartfelt - not the club, party, or typical record that everybody wanted. We even had a feeling that T.I. was gonna mention that, but we already had a plan for him." Personally, I wanted to find my home. I wanted the old version of myself to be indeed dead and gone, never to be remembered again. This long road traveled was weary, and I was tired of traveling on this journey alone. Little did I know, T.I, had the secret that I was searching for-- to be dead and gone. The old Lo needed to go and needed to let his old self die. If I wanted to experience true happiness, and discover the meaning of life, I needed to let go of my old habits and patterns. I needed to let all this be dead and gone, in order for me to truly live the life that was designed for me.

There I was on my bed, mind in a whirlwind, pondering the meaning of life, wondering why everything was falling apart, and questioning everything existing around me. My heart was broken, and my motivation was at an absolute zero. Just when I was at the peak of my thoughts, the phone rang. I reached for the phone and put it to my ear.

"Hey, what's up?"

It was my sister. "Nothin' much," she responded. "Just checkin' to see how you're doing."

I shot back the typical response, "All's good." It was a lie, not everything was okay, but our conversation continued as if it was.

A few minutes into our conversation, my sister informed me about a certain upcoming annual young adult conference that she was about to attend. This conference spanned over the New Year's weekend and drew crowds of young people together who wanted to begin the New Year with God.

"Dupa, you should come." (That was the nickname she always used for me. No, I won't explain what it means. LOL!) She continued to extend the invitation, "It'll be good. Plus, someone is sponsoring you. So, you don't even got to pay."

"Hmmm, sounds good, just let me know the details, and I'll go from there," I requested.

"So, this year, the conference is taking place in Louisville, Kentucky." My sister continued to share some more details for the next few minutes. I listened intently and considered her invitation. In the past, I had done a bit of traveling, and I enjoyed collecting hats from various cities. I weighed out the pros and cons, and finally concluded that it wasn't a bad idea to start the New Year on a spiritual note rather than spending the New Year recovering from a hangover. Plus, I figured that buying a hat from Louisville to add to my collection was a plus.

After fleshing out some of the trip details, I accepted my sister's invitation, "Yeah, sure, sis, count me in."

A few weeks after that phone call, the day came for me to leave for this conference. My sister directed me to meet her at the church, where everyone would load up on the busses and head out to Louisville. Still having little to no idea about this conference, I questioned myself. *What am I really getting myself into?* Despite the questioning going on in my head, I decided to trust my sister, because I knew she always had my best interest at heart when it came to my spiritual life.

The coach bus set for Louisville was parked at the far corner of the lot of the church. I made my way over to the bus and loaded my luggage on its bottom storage compartment. I was surrounded by commotion, tons of people were dropping off their kids or nieces and nephews. They were running around making sure all the details were squared away before the bus headed out. Most of the people stepping on to the bus were pre-teens. There were a few that appeared to be my age, but they seemed to be the chaperones for the trip.

Doubt crept in. *Do I really want to go to this thing? What did I get myself into?* The lot was filled with mostly unfamiliar faces with the exception of a few of the church members that I knew from my sister's church. And of course, there was my immediate family. Just as my thoughts regarding the weekend were being amplified with uncertainty and doubts, I spotted one of my boys, Kwame, from a distance.

"Yo Lo, what's up man?" I was stoked to see that Kwame was also attending this conference, or so I thought. We dapped and greeted each other and our conversation continued, but a few seconds into it, I realized that Kwame wasn't going to the conference after all.

"Yeah, man, just came to drop off the nephew. From what my mom told me, this conference is for little kids." All this just added to my cloud of doubts. "You goin'?" he asked.

"Yup," I responded rather self-consciously. I knew what he was thinking. *Lo-Ammi Richardson, the one who partied, clubbed, drank, smoked, and got into fights was actually going to this kid conference?*

At this point, my doubts started getting the best of me, and I decided that I wasn't going to go on this trip. *I'm not going to be looking stupid going to a conference with a bunch of jits!* I headed over to the bus luggage compartment to try to reclaim my bags, which by now, were sandwiched between random kid suitcases. I went to go talk to my brother-in law. As I was looking for him, my boy Mo saw me from a distance.

I AM > I WAS | 93

"Yoooooooooo, What's gooooood man?" That's all I heard being yelled over my direction. Mo was one of my homies that I had played ball with in the past and grew up in church with. He came over to greet me.

It had been years since I had seen him. I always appreciated him as a friend. He was always a straightforward guy who kept himself out of a lot of trouble. I respected him for that. I imagined that must have been hard for him to see a lot of our friends leave the church and pursue a life outside of it. But, he never seemed to judge us for it. From this church group, he was actually one of the very few consistent people that had a positive influence. That was Mo.

Mo was excited to see me and even more thrilled that I was attending this conference.

He asked how I was doing, and we caught up quickly. Mo had attended a Bible school in California. I was proud of him for taking that step and entering ministry. I expressed to him my doubts about attending this conference for little kids. He assured me that the conference wasn't for little kids after all, and that it was geared towards young adults my age. He continued to share with me his personal experience attending this conference and how it impacted him for the better. Mo encouraged me to give the conference a shot and not to back out on my plans.

That conversation shifted my thoughts about the conference. My doubts and hesitation towards attending were erased, and I decided to re-attend. Mo left me with these parting words, "I don't think you know what you're getting yourself into." Little did I know, those words would end up having a lasting effect on me. A few moments later, I was on the bus, heading to Louisville. As I stared out the window observing cars pass by, I couldn't help but ponder questions about life and myself and wonder what I was about to gain from this conference.

After a few stops for snacks and bathroom breaks, a couple hundred miles and several tired hours later, we finally arrived at our destination, the Louisville Convention Center. From there, we carried our luggage to the nearby hotel where we were all booked to stay for the weekend. As I stood at the center of the hotel lobby, waiting to check into my room, I couldn't help but notice the scene around me. While scanning my surroundings, I quickly realized that I didn't belong here. This was not my crowd. I didn't fit in. Everyone there looked corny. They all looked different from me, dressed differently, and even spoke differently. It was "God bless you brother, hallelujah sis, etc." left and right of me. There I stood with my fitted hat, baggy jeans and heavy varsity jacket feeling and looking like a fish out of water. The one thing that did stick out to me was that people around me just seemed genuinely happy and joyful.

Shortly after that awkward moment, the conference began, and I found my sister and brother-in-law, and hung out with them. The main scheduling framework of the conference consisted of a few general main meanings held at a large plenary hall and scattered in between were a variety of breakout sessions for us to choose from. I found a few seminars that piqued my interest, not because I wanted to learn spiritual things, but because I wanted to gain knowledge that would help me win debates with my friends.

A brother named Sebastien Braxton preached. When he spoke, I was locked in. The conference had a very intense schedule. It began at 6am and concluded at 9pm. Sebastien spoke at the 7am main session. I was never a morning person but waking up at this hour to listen to him was worth it. When he spoke, I related to him. His story seemed so similar to mine. He spoke with passion, conviction and was straight forward with his delivery. He didn't mince words at all. He wasn't defined by his past mistakes because he found something better to live for.

During his talks, I would sit in complete amazement. His talks would make me wonder, *Man, what does he have that I don't?* I grew up knowing this church stuff, yet, *why did I never have the passion for it the way that he does?*

Unlike Sebastien, I grew up in the church. He didn't grow up believing what I believed. However, when he discovered the truths that I had ingrained into me all my life, he became a changed man. *Why did those same truths impact him that way? And not me? With the passion and conviction he was preaching with, it seemed like he was willing to die for the truth that he was speaking.*

I wasn't ready to die for anything I was currently doing. Straight up. I'd witnessed some crazy things in my life. I was aware of my choice of lifestyle and the results it would bring. For certain, I wasn't interested in dying for any of those things. Yet, on the contrast, Sebastien had found something worth dying for. His words were exactly what I needed to hear in order to put my life into perspective. *What did I have that was worth dying for?*

Towards the end of the conference, my sister suggested that I go and meet some new people. (Just shows that sister-brotherly love, right? LOL!) I took her up on that suggestion and tried to make a few friends.

Friday evening was approaching, and everyone was busy getting their final things in order before night fall because stores were going to be closed on Saturday. I was standing in a crowded line waiting to order my food at a small bagel store, when I noticed a pretty girl standing next to me with a box a pizza. It was obvious that she was looking for a microwave to reheat the pizza. So, I started processing what to say to this pretty girl. After all, I was here to mingle, right? In my mind, I knew what I was going to say and how she was going to respond. However, to make a long story short, I failed. Miserably! I stuttered and stumbled over my words. It was a terrible first impression.

She must have been either graciously forgiving or completely forgetful, because even though I didn't make a good first impression at all, we did still end up having a super dope conversation. Her name was Stacy, and she told me a little about herself, along with her life story. I learned that we had something in common. That was, she had been in my same shoes the previous year, when she had attended this same conference for the first time. For Stacy the outcome of the conference was a life changer.

This was the first conversation that I had with anyone that was real, honest, and genuine.

Stacy was super down to earth, and I appreciated her for that. It was a dope encounter. After that, to my luck, I kept bumping into her everywhere I went for the remainder of the conference.

During this conference, at the main meetings, my family and I would always arrive to the large conference hall early so we could get good seats. Well, the following morning, our usual early seat hunting plan didn't work because I lost my sister and brother-in-law in the crowd. Now, I was all by my lonesome. The crowd was growing, seats were filling up, and I was surrounded by a sea of unfamiliar faces.

From a distance, I spotted a familiar face. It was Stacy. *I wonder if I can manage myself to sit next to her.* I thought. This was my opportunity, so, I figured I'd play it cool. Not wanting to come off as desperate, I knew I had to be strategic in my approach in trying to get her attention.

Stacy was sitting in the far left corner, about 7 rows from the stage. *I'll just look in her direction. Sit on the far right, about two rows in front of her, and pretend to be looking for someone.* This was my smooth, non-desperate looking, completely natural plan. By doing this, I was hoping that we'd *accidentally* make eye contact, she would then wave, and finally invite me to sit next to her.

I executed my plan, roaming innocently down the aisle and sitting in the specific seat as planned. Acting out the scene I had created in my mind, I turned and glanced in her direction. Plan failed! She was gone! Feeling stuck, I wasn't sure what to do next. Part of me didn't want to move from that spot because it was actually a good seat. However, I didn't want to sit there by myself.

The crowd continued to rush in, and the good seats were all disappearing. So, I remained in the seat I was in. Little did I know that this failed plan of attack, to sit next to Stacy, was all actually led by a hand of providence. The seat I was in, was exactly where I needed to be.

The program began with song service. Following that, the pastor walked on stage to preach his sermon. The pastor began talking as all other pastors and preachers do, but this time it was different. There was something about his message that spoke straight to my heart. It was as though I was the only one in the room, the single-sole person in the audience, as if the sermon was tailor made for me. Every question I had concerning the direction of my life, he answered directly. He spoke about destiny and purpose. He emphasized that we have a calling in our life. "There was no mistake. God has placed you in the position you are in." I was so overwhelmed by the message. I didn't know how to process everything I was hearing and feeling. For the first time, I felt this tug on my heart. My heart was filled with hope and a sense of love and happiness I had never felt before. *This* was what I was searching for. The very thing I desired to have I had found. Some may call it luck, others may deem it a coincidence, but to me it was providence. God seated me exactly where I needed to be. It was as if the very seat I was in had been previously reserved and had my name plastered all over it.

The pastor made an appeal towards the conclusion of his sermon. During the appeal, my eyes looked up and landed on my sister seated a distance away from me. That did it. I lost it. Tears streamed down my cheeks. Flashbacks of all the moments my sister prayed for played through my mind. I could see images of my mother on her knees whispering fervent prayers for me. They never gave up hope that one day I would actually get my act together and live out the purpose that was given to me.

It hit me like a ton of bricks. *I'm selfish. My actions hurt people close to me. I have been frontin' thinking that I had it all together, but in reality, my world was crumbling.* Two voices started speaking in my head. One told me to let go of the past and look forward towards a better future. The other voice warned me that if I were to do that, the cost would be great. I began battling with the decision of dying to my old self and letting go of the past–to start anew. As I was wrestling with these thoughts, my phone lit up with text messages and phone calls. My friends were wondering where I was. It was New Year's Eve and they were out drinking, partying, and having a blast. And there I was, crying like I just lost my mother, sitting in an auditorium full of young people, attending this Bible conference, debating whether or not I wanted to give up my old lifestyle.

That evening was a turning point. I made my decision and committed to starting a new kind of life, a life where I didn't allow my past to affect the person I desired to be. A life with God by my side. I left that conference a changed man–a man with a new perspective. The change wasn't easy. It wasn't even smooth sailing afterwards because old habits die hard. But over time, I was able to let go of those old habits. I was a new person.

The reason it was hard at first was because I didn't make a full-on commitment to the changes I wanted to make. I had a tendency to compromise. I told myself, I wouldn't drink to get drunk. I'd just drink to socialize. I would attend parties but not participate in dancing or fighting. But the more I tried, the more I realized it wasn't the same.

What I experienced at that conference was real and genuine. For the first time in my life I felt like I had a new start and perspective. The Old me was Dead and Gone! As T.I. said. The freedom I experienced, knowing that the old me is gone is something I cannot put into words. The freedom of knowing that I can be made new and have a new start in life is something everyone can experience. No one is defined by their past nor their mistakes or shortcomings. You are who you decide to be today. There were moments in my life that

I felt like what T.I. said on the hook of his song, "Dead and Gone."

There is someone greater than you, who is looking out for you. You are never alone. But the reason why we don't allow the old man to die, or why we don't see the people who are by our side is because of pride. Don't let pride get in the way of your new chapter. You can have a fresh start today.

I can honestly say I'm free! I'm the happiest I've ever been, not because life became easy but because I now know who I am, why I'm here, and where I am going. I want the same for you!

I'm glad the old me is dead and gone.

QUESTIONS

- Have you experienced a new start in your life? If not, what is hindering you from starting a new life and dying to the old you?
- How does pride get in the way from taking the step needed to leave the old life behind and start a new chapter in your life?
- Has there been someone in your life that has helped guide you towards the path you needed to go? If so, who? If not, then can you identify people in your circle who have been positive influences? What are the positive influences they have made in your life?
- Why is it hard to let go of the past and embrace the future?

CHAPTER 10

IF THEY COULD ONLY SEE ME NOW!

My journey since the youth conference has been amazing. Don't get me wrong, life is still hard. There is no way around that fact. People may say it's all about happiness and living your best life now, which is true. However, this life will still bring on unexpected hardships, no matter what.

So, how does one get around all this? By focusing on the big picture and setting necessary goals. Doing this makes all the difference, for it creates a safety net. This way, those hiccups in life won't be able to stop you from pursuing your calling and establishing your identity. Above all, the most important thing to remember is that if you are experiencing the hardships of life, keep in mind that you don't have to stay living in that experience. You have the ability to turn those hardships into something positive.

In the past, I have made many mistakes. I've blown money, experienced heartbreak, partied, clubbed, drank, smoked, sold drugs, got into fights and countless other things. Though my past may not have been the best, I made a conscious decision to turn those negatives into positives. From those former experiences, I gleaned the tools to help others learn. Because of those mistakes, I am able to share firsthand that it's possible to not let mistakes define you, and also provide tangible evidence that forming a new reality is possible.

Since making the decision to *die to the old man*, life has thrown me its share of difficulties. Since that time, I've lost both my mother and father. I've experienced heartbreaks. My reputation has been smeared by those who claimed to care and love me. But, despite these things, something still keeps me going. What is it? My purpose! Because I now have purpose, all these setbacks in life, don't have to become roadblocks to my success anymore. I now live to fulfill what I was created to be. I've realized that the hardships and setbacks of life can't prevent me from reaching my goals and hindering me from accomplishing my dreams.

What are the things I want to accomplish? I want to see my friends experience a different, better, and more fulfilling life. I aspire to impact my community in a way that leaves a positive influence. I wish to leave a legacy of change. In the end, I know that during my stay on earth I helped to make things better.

The most gratifying thought during my entire journey of change, is knowing that my friends, who have known me from the jump, have been able to witness the positive changes I have made in my life. These are the same friends who were bystanders during my hustling, cursing, partying, drug-selling, fighting, and other crazy antic-filled years. Today, these same friends are able to witness my travels around the world as I share my story of becoming an overcomer.

These people from my past, they are my motivation. They are who keep me continually rolling and striving for my purpose. They are my why. I do it for them––the friends who need to see that change is possible, my family who believed in me during the moments even I couldn't believe in myself, the community that's seeking for hope, and God who never gave up on me throughout the process.

While I was attending a Bible college, I had a conversation on the phone with my boy Fred. I will never forget our conversation. As we were catching up, he asked me, "Lo, what caused you to make the changes you've made?" Fred knew me well. We had lived together. We hustled together. We shared, what we coined, *Jesus moments*. This was the term we used for moments when life got hard, and things didn't go as planned. During these times, we'd experience a glimpse of Jesus, and remember to pray, read the Bible, and attend church. Unfortunately, as soon as our situation would improve, we reverted back to our old habits.

So, when Fred finally saw me having the ultimate *Jesus moment*, he waited, expecting me to revert back to my old way of living. However, this time, he noticed I didn't. When this happened, he asked, "How is it that you've been so consistent? How did you make those changes and actually stick with them?" I struggled trying to provide an answer as eloquently as a pastor would. Fred stopped me and told me that I sounded like a preacher, instead of one of his homeboys. He asked me to just be straight up with him.

Pausing briefly to think about his question again, I responded, "I don't know. I don't know what caused me to stay and make that change. All I knew was that after that weekend in Kentucky, I had questions that I needed to find answers to. Once I got all the answers I needed, I was compelled to make a change, and I did."

Fred's next few words have stuck with me to this very day. He commented, "I respect that, and just know that we (my friends) are looking at you from a distance. If you ever decide to go back to doing what you were doing before, you would be welcomed back with open arms. But the day that you do, just know you killed your witness about God towards me."

What words! What motivation! I stick with my change for people like him! I do it for all my friends and the people I come in contact with, those who want to make changes in their lives but are too afraid to do so because they can't see any other alternatives. When my life was a mess, no one was around to truly show me it was possible to actually climb out of the ditches and make positive change. Neither did the people I rolled with have that example as well. Yes, we were told to make changes, but where was the living proof that it was actually possible? It was as if it was just talk, and as a result we were constantly stuck in our own messy cycles of life. To those seeking to make a positive change, I can say that it is possible. I did it. And so can you. I'm living proof.

Many people out there share my same experience. They desire to make life changes, but it's discouraging for them because they don't see walking evidence that change is possible and worth it. Where are the other living examples? Where are those people that have overcome hardships, adversity and have proven that things such as culture, stereotypes, or mistakes don't have to define them? If you are reading this, and you are also a living example of positive change. Step out there. Share your story. Be someone's motivation. You may just be someone's lifesaver.

Since that pivotal moment at the conference in 2009, my life has never been the same. Since then, I have understood my purpose. I now better understand my calling. I know why I have been placed on this earth and what my mission in life should be. Since then, there have been so many incredible experiences I have had since making the decision to change my life. This book doesn't have room to include them all.

Since 2009, I've had the privilege of being a chaplain for various academies. I've had the honor of traveling all around the country and overseas to places such as Haiti, Canada, Africa, Taiwan, Philippines, Lebanon, and even Hawaii. At those places, I've shared my experience of what God has done since the moment I found my identity in Him. Oh, I know that my friends from the past, probably view my talks online, and think to themselves, "That's, Lo?!"

A former college dropout to now a college graduate, I became the first person in my immediate family to graduate from college. Both my parents weren't able to accomplish this milestone, neither were they able to witness my graduation since they had both passed by that time. Oh, if they could just see me now with my diploma in hand! I can only imagine the smiles plastered on their faces.

Obviously, the fact that you are reading this book means that I am a published author. Along with that, I have had the privilege to be one of the directors of SALT (Service and Love Together), an organization that focuses on city missions and impacting the local community by caring for the poor and ministering to the urban youth in low income communities. SALT became the first organization to create the Change Trailer (think of it as Goodwill on wheels), which brought clothes and toiletries to homeless friends. It was also the first organization in Central Florida to own and operate a shower trailer for these same homeless friends. In order to make this trailer possible, SALT achieved a huge financial goal of raising 40k. How? By seeing the vision and executing that vision. That vision can only be achieved when you know what you have been called to do.

Today, more than ever, I realize I can't implement change if I don't change. I cannot continue to be defined by things around me. I have to live up to what I was created to be. Who would have thought that the same mouth that got me into trouble is now the mouth that is used to share positivity and purpose for others to hear? My former teachers, I hope they see me now, and end up nothing short of shocked and surprised Because now, instead of causing havoc in classrooms, I help the people who lost their identity find it once again. Many of these are lost high school students like me years ago.

I never realized that my talent and purpose was to speak, but once I discovered it, I've used it to impact the world. It's amazing to know that my mother always believed in me. She never lost hope that one day I would reach my potential. She saw something I didn't see in myself. If she were still alive, I know she would be proud of me.

Why am I sharing all this? To show you what can happen once you dream big! Once you understand your purpose, lock into your identity, and understand what you have been created to be, then nothing can stop you from dreaming big and accomplishing monumental dreams and goals.

Once you are locked into who you are, what your purpose is and what dreams you have set for yourself, people will invest in it. After I made the choice to change my life, I had no clue of the adventure awaiting around the corner. You too can do the same!

Many have chosen to define or categorize me as a thug, misfit, or rebel after they've learned about my life story. Yes, perhaps my behavior did match some of those labels, but I never let them define me. Don't let others define you. Remember, you aren't defined by your past or mistakes. You are defined by what you know you have been created to be.

Seek your passions. Develop your goals. Discover who you have been created to be.

Do you love to write? If so, then write your story for the world to read. Enjoy singing? Compose music that will bring happiness to listeners. Into building and design? Then create something useful and innovative that will impact lives in a positive way. Have hoop dreams? Use those God-given talents to inspire and create opportunities for others such as Lebron did for his city.

That's what I want from you. I want you to use your God-given talents to impact our world. You have an influence that nobody else has. You have a unique set of talents and gifts personally crafted for you to do things that only you can do. You can be the example of change that people are clamoring to witness.

One of my favorite quotes I strive to live by states, "Success in any line demands a definite aim. He who would achieve true success in life must keep steadily in view of the aim worthy of his endeavor. Such an aim is set before the youth of today!"

This success came about when I had the opportunity to share my story on stage, before thousands of people, and more via live television. I shared my story at the very same conference that changed my life. Before my mom passed away, she was able to witness her boy preaching on that stage, living up to the talent she knew he had possessed all the while. Though even I was surprised that I had this chance of a lifetime, my mom wasn't. Why? Because, this whole time, she knew who I was created to be.

Mama was proud I had finally found my identity and my calling. That opportunity to come full circle and be a motivational speaker at the same conference that changed my life was an incredible experience. There I was living up to my God given potential. I want the same for you. If God saw something in me, I have no doubt that He sees something in you. That's why I wrote this book, to make that message clear to you.

I realized that I am much more than my mistakes. I was designed to implement change and encourage others to do the same. I am the son of a King! That's who I am. That's what I have been created to be. If only they could see me now!

QUESTIONS

- What have you been designed to be? What do you feel is your talent and God-given purpose here on earth?
- Have you had experiences in your life (good or bad) that have caused you to realize your purpose? If so, what were they?
- How have you handled the mistakes in your past? What can you do to channel those past mistakes into something positive today?
- Reflect and think about your current situation and your life story. Ask yourself the question, "Who am I?" Once you have answered that question, ask yourself, is this who I want to be? If not, what changes in your life need to be made in order for you to become the person that you were designed to be?

ABOUT THE AUTHOR

Lo-Ammi was born in a Christian home, but after high school, he pursued a career in basketball, and got caught up in hip-hop, drugs, alcohol, and violence, being arrested various times as a juvenile. After God led him to attend a Youth Conference in Kentucky, his life changed forever. His passion is to see young people find their purpose and help young people utilize their God given passion to make an impact in their local community and around the world.

Lo-Ammi is a world renown International Speaker and Revivalist. He is an advocate for mental health and social justice and has used his talents to orchestrate projects that included a Kid's Tutoring program for lower income communities and help with special projects to help combat homelessness in the Orlando area.

Lo-Ammi is a graduate from Oakwood University (HBCU) and has a Bachelors in Church Leadership. He loves to travel, play basketball, read and does photography and vlogging as a hobby in his free time.

WWW.LOAMMIRICHARDSON.COM

www.ingramcontent.com/pod-product-compliance
Lightning Source LLC
Chambersburg PA
CBHW062034120526
44592CB00036B/2104